D1409925

GAME DAY

GAME DAY

A ROLLICKING JOURNEY TO THE HEART OF COLLEGE FOOTBALL

CRAIG JAMES

WILEY

John Wiley & Sons, Inc.

Published by John Wiley & Sons, Inc., Hoboken, New Jersey
Published simultaneously in Canada

Library of Congress Cataloging-in-Publication Data:

James, Craig, date.
   Game day : a rollicking journey to the heart of college football/Craig James.
      p.   cm.
   Includes index.
   ISBN 978-0-470-47056-5 (cloth)
      1. Football–United States. 2. College sports–United States. I. Title.
   GV950.J36   2009
   796.332'63—dc22
                                                          2009015964

Printed in the United States of America
10 9 8 7 6 5 4 3 2 1

Dedicated to the men and women of the military, who serve our country with fierce pride, bravery, and dedication, allowing us the freedoms we have as Americans. Thank you!

CONTENTS

ACKNOWLEDGMENTS

There is no way this book or my broadcasting career would have been possible without having a strong, loving wife taking care of our family while I was gone. Thank you, Marilyn.

Nor would all of this have been possible without my four great kids, Jessica, Caylin, Adam, and Andy, who are also outstanding people. I never once had to worry about them while I was on the road. Thanks for your support, understanding, and love.

Thanks also to my mom, Nancy, and step-dad, Charlie Vickers, for making sure I always had a glove, bat, and cleats. And to my dad, Will "Pete" James, thanks for demanding that I work as hard as possible to be the best I could be at whatever I did.

As for this book, I want to acknowledge my agent, Frank R. Scatoni of Venture Literary, for his guidance and help in making this a reality. Many thanks to Stephen S. Power and John Simko from John Wiley & Sons for helping to make this book what it is.

Most important, thanks to my Lord and savior Jesus Christ for giving me one incredible ride.

WHY I LOVE THIS GAME

I believe it was the 1992 season while doing a Saturday College Football ESPN scoreboard show when Tim Brando decided to nickname me the "Pony." Brando's one of the more talented announcers I've ever worked with. He's full of bull most of the time, but he loves college football—and that passion comes across to the fans. I guess Tim figured that since I played for the SMU Mustangs and that my teammate Eric Dickerson and I were referred to as "the Pony Express," my new name should be the Pony. The name stuck and has paved the way for some pretty interesting conversations along the way.

Like the time I was covering a Rose Bowl, and before the game started, I made my way to the restroom. I was standing there doing my business when this fan in the urinal next to me yelled out, "I always wanted to know why they called you the Pony!" I didn't know whether to punch him or laugh! He then pointed his cell phone camera at me and took a picture. Being surrounded by tons of fans, there wasn't a thing I could do about it. As a result of that encounter, I'm a lot more careful where I go to use the restroom!

While this experience sticks out a little more than others, my years of covering college football have been extremely rewarding —in large part due to the relationship I've built with you, the fan. I've met tons of wild and crazy fans—which is part of why I love this game so much. There's so much energy, so much passion. On any given Saturday, millions of die-hards from all over the country get to see dozens of incredible matchups—with conference and national championships on the line week in and week out. And, lucky for me, I've got one of the best seats in the house.

One thing's for certain in my life: as my Rose Bowl restroom encounter shows, I'm never lonely for conversation. Whether I'm at the grocery store, getting gas, eating out, you name the place, more than likely there will be a fan or a group of fans ready to pipe in about their school and why they should be number 1.

What I've found is that I could say nine good things about a school, and the fan will remember my only negative comment. My friend and colleague John Saunders has this theory that fans are used to seeing us all the time on TV and feel as if they really know us, so it's no big deal to come up to us and tell us what's on their minds.

That's fine with me, because when that happens, I know I'm connecting with you—and that's what I'm paid to do and what I love to do. For many years I've believed that it's my responsibility to work hard and be prepared when I go on the air. True, I do work for ESPN/ABC, but in the end, I'm really partners with the college football fan.

●　　●　　●

I've loved college football since my first day of practice as a freshman at Southern Methodist University (SMU). I didn't grow up as a high-maintenance kid *expecting* to play beyond high school, so I probably enjoyed and appreciated my playing days more than most athletes. Plus, I had the mind-set that I was going to work as hard as I could in order to maximize my God-given talent. I didn't want to ever look back on my career as a football player and wish that I'd done more to take advantage of and fully develop my abilities. It's the same thing I tell my kids about their time in sports and the same speech I give other athletes when sharing my experiences. I often remind players that character is defined as what you do when nobody is watching.

As an athlete, it means that when you're by yourself and scheduled to run ten 100-yard sprints on a particular workout, then run ten—especially on the day when you really want to stop at eight. Now, a coach wouldn't have known if you or I had skipped out on two sprints. But the most important person would have known we shortchanged our workout: you and me! I would have known deep down inside—and it would have bothered the heck out of me. I'm a big believer that if you let the little things slide, big issues will show up to challenge you. Another example of personal discipline (and it might sound corny, but players will know exactly what I'm talking about here): My freshman year at SMU our head trainer, Cash Birdwell, told a group of us that carbonation from soda was bad for you and would cut your wind. Cash said it was better to drink a beer than a soda. Unfortunately, we took his advice to heart and tested the cold beer theory! I was eighteen years old when I heard that from Cash, and didn't have a carbonated drink until I retired from football ten years later. At some point in time I realized it wouldn't really hurt my wind while running, but it was a personal discipline that I had adopted, and I didn't want to "let up." I suppose by not letting up I was able to maximize my talents in football, creating more than a joyride for a guy out of East Texas.

The James gang comes from a small East Texas farming community: Alto, Texas, in Cherokee County, better known back in the day as the Tomato Capitol of the World. I grew up as a little boy either riding on the heater vent in the school bus next to my grandfather—the school bus driver—or sitting next to my dad on a tractor, plowing a field. I used to love riding the pastures and feeding the cows or going into the garden and picking the biggest tomato in the patch. My grandfather called the big ones "hoochers." It sounds a little goofy now, but believe me when I tell you that it was fun—kind of like an Easter egg hunt, except all of 'em were red. So the goal was to find the biggest.

As a football player, I was lucky to have been on some really good football teams. And because of our teams' successes, I was able to achieve several personal highlights that have followed me to this day.

One of my fondest memories as a player dates back to my earliest playing days. I started playing football when I was in the third grade. I played on the Redskins. Man, we were good. I wore number 55 and was a linebacker/quarterback—when you're that age, you play on both sides of the ball, since the game isn't as specialized as it is once you get a little older. I remember the night before a big game against the Browns as well as I do the night before the Super Bowl when I played with the New England Patriots against the Chicago Bears in 1986. Trying to go to sleep that night as a ten-year-old boy was next to impossible. I was in bed, acting like it was the Washington Redskins and Cleveland Browns of the NFL about to square off on a Saturday morning in Texas—and that I was either a star running back or linebacker. Say what you want about visualization, but I can tell you that I saw myself playing in the NFL that night (of course, what kid doesn't?), and I knew that only hard work and dedication would get me there. But I will admit that at the age of ten, I'm not sure I'd have been so willing to give up soda!

From before the days of handheld video cameras, etched in my mind is a long TD run I made up the middle of the field. We played on a combination baseball/football field, so it had dirt in the middle—just like the old NFL stadiums that had dual-use fields. I thought I was the next Jim Brown that day, so you can imagine what it was like for me later in life to actually play against the Redskins and the Browns. I scored my first professional touchdown at RFK Stadium against the 'Skins, and I was fortunate to have played the Browns in their original stadium.

Man, that Browns stadium was old—and the visitors' locker room was a *long* way from our sideline. So far away that by the time we'd get to the locker room, we had to turn around and go back. And the shower room was dirty as all get-out! I was a neat freak about showers and usually packed my flip-flops to walk around the visitors' locker room, but unfortunately I forgot to pack them that week. I showered standing on my heels so my toes wouldn't touch the floor.

I also remember singing the national anthem prior to the kickoff of those games—a rookie in the NFL, but still a little boy inside. I had tears in my eyes thinking back on my youth football game as a Redskin.

Today, the game of football is mostly about speed. Gone are the days—like in the '90s—when the Nebraska Cornhuskers could just jam the ball down your throat. Teams like the University of Florida are recruiting players who can win in space, guys who can make plays in the open field without help from a teammate. I hear coaches talk all the time about matchups and how they try to get "their guy" one-on-one with a defender. A great example is the Gators' speedy multithreat player, Percy Harvin. I don't care how good of a defensive call you make, guys like Harvin will beat you with speed and ability.

Here's another example: If you want to see pure talent and ability on display, rewatch the 2009 Fiesta Bowl between Texas and Ohio State. Buckeyes QB Terrell Pryor was bottled up time and again, yet he would escape, using his speed, to make a big play and keep the Buckeyes in the game. If not for Pryor, Ohio State would have had no shot at winning that game. As it turns out, they would have won, if not for a heroic final-minute march downfield by Colt McCoy and the Longhorns.

That was just one of the games in the 2008 bowl season that had me on the edge of my seat. The game has gotten so much more exciting lately, with much more parity in each of the conferences. No doubt a large reason for parity has come about with the ceiling placed on total scholarships per year—a school has twenty-five scholarships to give out each year. That's a far cry from the pre-1980s–era when big powerhouse state schools could sign as many players as they wanted to and give a scholarship to practically everyone who had talent. This strategy was a way for these particular schools to sign up all of the good players and thereby keep their competition from getting any decent prospects. There sure wasn't a lot of character in the coaches back then, when they'd tell a kid this and that just to get them to sign, and then kill the kid's hopes and dreams once he arrived on campus only to find out that there weren't enough spots on an active roster to go around for all the talent sitting on the bench. But not anymore.

With fewer scholarships per school, the smaller-budget programs are able to get some pretty darn nice players. So take this spread-the-love and limited-scholarships approach and add to it better coaching, and you've just described a formula for parity. No doubt, the coaching has gotten better because the money's gotten better. Heck, not long ago assistant coaches were making $30,000 to $40,000 a year. Now it's six figures for the most part and up to a half-million dollars a year just for the coordinators. I'd give you a number of head coaches out of the 119 Division 1-A schools making a million or more *per year*, but that number goes up with each new signing, so it's hard to keep the number current.

When I retired from the Patriots I could have stayed in the NFL as an assistant coach. I had no doubt whatsoever that I would have been a good coach. I knew the game and was able to communicate well with my teammates. But my wife, Marilyn, and I didn't want to subject our family to moving around every four or five years, as most coaches have to do—not for the amount of money being paid at that time.

But I have to admit that if I were retiring today, with salaries being as high as they are, coaching would be a big-time consideration for me—just like it is for a lot of former players who've decided to enter coaching after their playing days are over.

In addition to the money and the fact that the talent pool is so deep, you've also got these assistants spending time in both college and the NFL, so they're able to learn a ton more from some excellent coaches—and that only makes them better. Great examples are Pete Carroll of USC and Nick Saban at Alabama—they've been around both and have a distinct strategic advantage over coaches who've seen only one level. The NFL is graduate school for assistant coaches. They learn how to pick up opponents' tendencies quicker, how to coach techniques better to their players, how to disguise defensive looks better—all of which, when around the college game, makes the coach and, therefore, the team better. I'm more impressed with former defensive guys who turn college than I am offensive ones. Will Muschamp is a good example of a defensive coordinator who was doing really well as a college coach. Then in 2005 he went to the Miami Dolphins as a defensive coach and, in my opinion, honed his skills even more. Muschamp rejoined the college game and during my spring tour of 2008, I watched Muschamp at the University of Texas teach his defense the art of how to time a blitz. Texas felt they'd had a weakness with their timing in previous seasons, so they were working hard to perfect it. The idea is that even before the ball is snapped, a defense is showing a particular look. It could be a very basic alignment, yet right at the snap of the ball the players scatter and run a completely different blitz or scheme than was shown prior to the snap. By showing their hand late, the defense limits the ability of the offense to make adjustments with their blocking schemes. You see it all the time: the ball is snapped, and a defender comes flying by the offensive line and sacks the QB or tackles the ball carrier in the backfield. More times than not this is a result of great timing by the defense and by their not showing their hand too early. When an NFL QB is able to determine before the snap what a defense is running, it will be a very long day for that defense. So coaches in the NFL are forced to learn how to mask their intentions. I remember that as a running back in the NFL it was critical for me to have a pre-snap read of the defense, too. A tricky defense affects more than just the QB.

So combine scholarship limits with better coaching—and the advent of the spread offenses—and you've got parity. Spread offenses frustrate big, powerful defenses because of all of the formation changes and quick timing routes by the receivers. In short, the offense is giving multiple looks to the defense, causing the defenders to use their eyes a lot to see what the offense is trying to do. When you get defenders to use their eyes more than their feet, they aren't nearly as productive. One of the all-time upsets in college football happened in 2007. Little old Appalachian State visited the Big House and beat Michigan. It was a combination of good coaching, the spread offense, and a bunch of Appalachian State players who wanted to prove something to the big guys of Michigan, prove to them they weren't too small or slow or short as they'd been told when coming out of high school.

Because of these spread offenses, there has been a heavy emphasis on speed in the college game. Being an old man now (as my kids say), I can look back on my childhood and better appreciate the things I did as a youngster that helped develop my motor skills. I had some natural speed and was quick as a kid, and I wasn't afraid to either hit you or get hit. I wasn't afraid of anything.

I probably got that aggressive instinct from playing pickup ball in the yard with my younger brother, Chris, and friends. We'd team up with guys older than us, which forced us to either man up or go home. I tore up a lot of jeans and socks in those days and got lots of pinches from my mom for ruining my clothes while playing football. I didn't care, though. I loved playing.

Chris and I would even play one-on-one if we couldn't find anybody else. I suppose Chris would say that getting knocked around the yard was good for him, too. He was a good football player and signed a scholarship to play at SMU with me. But Chris decided that ice bags and bumps were the wrong path for him, so he chose to play baseball instead, which was a very good decision: he went on to play ten years of major league baseball. His football background stayed with him, though, as he had a reputation as a hardass. As a matter of fact, one year the San Diego Padres gave him the "Red Ass" award. Bro would get in your face in a second if he thought you were dogging it or not giving it your all. He still does, actually, and that's why baseball management loved him. Chris didn't need motivating to play hard—and his work ethic motivated and inspired teammates. He was a great clubhouse guy to have around. Incidentally, the trophy his Padres teammates gave him was a statue of a donkey.

I have to say that one difference between my brother and me is that I'm more politically correct and aware of what I should or shouldn't do—but the same competitive red blood flows through both of us.

Chris and I talk all the time about it—about how today's kids just don't seem to have that burning desire to excel. Maybe kids are more sheltered today. I can promise you we weren't protected. Up until I was about nine, we spent a lot of time in the country. Chris and I would saw off the end of a broom so we could use the stick as a bat. The two of us would stand in a field and hit rocks into a pasture. No telling how many rocks we'd pick up and hit. Then, for a break, we'd find an old mop to use between our legs and run around the yard like we were riding a horse. Doing stuff like that at a young age is how we developed our speed and skills. There wasn't any Wii or Xbox to play with, that's for sure.

As I think back on my third-grade season (my first year of football), a couple of things stand out. First, four or five days before a regular-season game, I badly cut my thumb and had to go to the emergency room for stitches. I was sitting on the table with the doctor trying to sew my thumb up and screaming pretty loudly. Crazy, isn't it, to think a ten-year-old would cry over stitches. Well, my dad didn't like my insanity too much, so he decided to smoke me in the kisser with his fist. Dad, at 6 foot 3 and 250 pounds, told me to shut up and let the doctor do his work! Obviously my dad and the doctor didn't believe in a shot to deaden the area! I sat still and let the man do his thing.

Leaving the emergency room, I was told not to play in my upcoming football game. Goofy doctor didn't learn much after seeing my dad nail me, did he? That Saturday morning I was dressed and playing in my game. Right before halftime, I was tackled and got up to see blood all over my hand. My stitches had been blown out. Dad came over to the bench, grabbed my arm, and told me to come with him. We went to the parking lot where he reached in the tool box for his black electrical tape. Dad wound that tape around my thumb so tight the blood stopped flowing. He threw the tape back in the truck and told me to get my butt back in the game!

As you might suspect, a lot of parents thought Dad was being an idiot. I probably thought so, too. But Dad did me a huge favor that day. He knew my life wasn't being threatened by going back in the game. His lesson that day taught me a lot about playing with pain. Many times throughout my football career I thought

11

back on that pee wee game when I'd get banged up—like the first play of the game against the Green Bay Packers in 1985. I got hit in the chin by a helmet, and it exploded with blood. I didn't miss a snap the entire first half. And at halftime, while getting stitches without any local anesthetic, I was laughing inside at the memory of that valuable lesson I learned many seasons earlier.

Later that season, I remember playing in the city championship and losing. I don't remember much of the game—I think I blocked it out—but I do remember crying afterward. I made up some excuse like I'd hurt my ankle, but the truth was that I hated losing and we hadn't lost all year. When I got older, tears turned to determination, and every time we lost, I pushed myself even harder to make more of an impact the next time we played that team. As a youngster, I didn't fully appreciate or understand how important a competitive streak is in your journey toward becoming a professional athlete. There's no doubt in my mind that my brother and I achieved professional status due in large part to the type of upbringing we had. We were taught to work hard and to respect our elders. To say "Please" and "Thank you" and to look adults in the eye and say "Yes, ma'am" and "Yes, sir."

Heck, we still compete against each other. We both recently took up bow hunting. I harvested my first buck the first deer season. Chris didn't, and it drove him nuts that I had one and he didn't. Of course, it didn't help that I ran around calling myself Davy Crockett.

There's an old saying that you're either hard or soft—my brother and I had nothing to do with being soft. We were country tough with a lot of drive and ambition.

Hands down, the most enjoyable athletic phase of my life was during my high school days. We were a bunch of like-minded, hard-working guys who set a goal our freshman year to win the state championship. A lot of my core beliefs were born from speeches made by our head coach, Oscar Cripps. Coach stressed how much can be accomplished when nobody cares who gets the credit. Coach was so crazy about the team concept that he hardly ever used the word "I"—and I'm not saying that to be cliché, that there's no "I" in "team." Coach really lived this philosophy, and if you weren't a team player, you had better become one or find a different after-school activity. To this day, I still pause or think about it when I use the word "I."

I'm still in touch with some of my high school teammates. We were a bunch of cutups back then, and we still are today. One of the better memories for me, and probably for a lot of my teammates, was the time I pulled a joke on our offensive coordinator, Bob French. He was a chump to most of us, a young buck who had a temper and wanted to control everything.

Well, Coach French decided that he'd had enough of a crappy practice one day, and he told us that the next player he saw with a foot on the field who wasn't supposed to be on the field was going to get his butt busted. There were probably twenty of us standing along the chalked sidelines. We were in Houston on a hot and really humid day. From a side view, all you could see were forty football cleats nudged right up next to the chalk line—make that thirty-nine shoes. I took off one of my cleats and had it six inches on the field.

"Sweet Old" Bob French ("SOB," as we called him) looked down the line to see if anybody had messed up. He came running down there to see this empty shoe. Coach SOB had the typical coach's body: skinny legs, no butt, and a big gut. French looked up at me and my laughing face and said, "Your ass is mine!"

I got three serious swats after practice. French tried to break the board on my butt, but couldn't. I sucked it up, looked him in the face, smiled, and walked out of the office like it didn't hurt. My teammates loved me for doing it. And when I got home to check out my buttocks, it was a welt. Thirty years later, when I see French, we laugh about me messing with him and how it really was funny as heck. Ultimately, I think Coach French and I both look back on it now and realize that our team having fun was probably the key to our winning the state championship. I see it all the time with teams—they all work so hard and have so much pressure on them from their parents, coaches, and peers that they forget that sports are supposed to be fun.

Coaches weren't our only targets. I'm not sure my high school teammate Chris Jackson would agree, but one of the better pranks we pulled was on him. Jackson was a good player who started on the offensive line as a junior. He later went on to SMU and was our starting center there. No doubt he was feeling his oats, so we decided to humble him. A group of seniors ganged up on him, stripped him down to his underwear, and tied him up with tape. We then took him outside our locker room where the drill team was working out. We dumped Jackson right in front of the best-looking girls in the school. Probably scarred him for life, but we sure got a heck of a laugh out of it and it did trim his ego a little bit.

The Houston Stratford Spartans, my high school team, was the best football team I ever played on. To this day, my teammates and I stay in touch and are really close. I was named Player of the Year in 1978 for the state of Texas after rushing for a state record 2,411 yards. I also scored 35 touchdowns that year, as our team went 15–0 and won the state championship, making our freshman-year pledge a reality.

One of the first big life decisions high school graduates have to make is where they are going to college. Or what they're going to do with their life. I knew I was going to college to play football, but I had a little twist to think about during the recruiting process. The summer before my sophomore year in high school, I met this beautiful blonde named Marilyn Arps. I was whipped from the first time I saw her, and she later became my wife. She was also the drum major on the drill team and thought I was an idiot for embarrassing Jackson. Oh, well, it served as a warning to her that I wasn't a boring stiff. Anyway, Marilyn was a year ahead of me in school—so I now say she's older than me. We've already passed the twenty-five-year anniversary mark.

Well, her sister Cindy was attending SMU, so Marilyn decided to go there, too. Needless to say, SMU had the inside track from day one. As soon as SMU offered me a scholarship before my senior season started, I jumped all over it and said yes. Head coach Ron Meyer and offensive coordinator Steve Endicott then started to wonder if I was any good. Their rationale? Why would a blue-chipper commit to lowly SMU so quickly? It didn't take Ron or Steve long to figure out why.

In college at SMU, my teammate was future first-ballot NFL Hall of Famer Eric Dickerson. Eric and I accounted for more than 9,000 yards between us. And because of those numbers, the Pony Express will live forever.

Man, Eric was a baller. He could flat-out play football. The first time Eric and I met was during our senior year of high school. We grew up thirty minutes from each other but were in different districts and classifications. Eric was in a smaller 2A district and I was in a big 4A district. We followed each other through the Houston papers, though, because we were the two highest-profile running backs in the state—a state, mind you, that is rabid about high school football. (Just read Buzz Bissinger's classic book, *Friday Night Lights*, to know what I'm talking about. That book is so good they made a movie and a TV series based on it.)

So here I am driving out to Sealy, Texas, to see the big man in person. I went by his house, and he wasn't there; they told me he was up at the car wash. I made my way through the small town and found Eric in the wash stall putting a shine to his Trans

Am—a gold one nonetheless. "Dick," as we later called him in school, was tall and skinny with a big ol' fro. His hair was almost as tall as he was. I crack up just thinking about the first time I laid eyes on Dick. And then, to top it off, Dick blares out to me: "Man, I thought you were a black dude! White guys can't run like you!"

Then he smiled, and we both started laughing our butts off. Little did either of us know at the time that we would go on to be forever linked together as the Pony Express. Nor did we know that, even more important than our football recognition, we'd become lifelong friends. I love Eric to this day and am glad to call him a friend. I was so proud of him the day he was inducted into the Hall of Fame. That tall, skinny kid at the car wash in Sealy went on to become one of the all-time great running backs in the history of the NFL. I'll never forget the run he made our sophomore year at Texas Stadium against the Arkansas Razorbacks. It was a pretty simple downhill run toward the right tackle. The defense jammed up that side of the line, so Eric stopped on a dime and cut back to the left. He went from stop to full speed straight ahead before the defense was able to even react to his initial cut. No telling how many ankles he sprained on that run. I knew then that number 19 was a special talent.

Fast-forward to our second year of pro football. Eric was playing for the Los Angeles Rams, and I was with the New England Patriots. We were out west in LA getting ready for a second-round playoff game against the Los Angeles Raiders. The Rams were playing on Saturday, and we were playing on Sunday. So I called Eric and told him I was coming to his game against the Dallas Cowboys. Imagine, if you will, me and a few of my Patriots teammates sitting in the stands at another pro football game the afternoon before we were to play the Raiders. I was like a kid cheering for his brother, and Eric nailed the Cowboys for 241 yards rushing. Unbelievable!

The next day we beat the Raiders. I called Eric, and we talked about how cool it would be if we both won our next games, which would set up a showdown of the Pony Express in a Super Bowl. We beat the Miami Dolphins to advance, but the Rams couldn't get by the Chicago Bears. Two weeks later, neither did we. I was bummed that Eric and I didn't get that chance to square off in the Super Bowl—that would have been storybook material. Regardless, it was a privilege to play with him.

For those of you too young to remember Eric Dickerson, check out YouTube. A few diehard fans have put up some tributes, and you can see for yourself just how great a runner he was.

The highlight of my professional career was playing in Super Bowl XX with the New England Patriots against the Chicago Bears. We got beat up pretty bad, but it was an honor to play on the biggest stage in all of professional sports. Two years earlier, in 1984, I made the NFL All Rookie team and was voted to the Pro Bowl as an alternate. In 1985, I started in the Pro Bowl, was voted the Patriots MVP, and was named the NFL's Offensive Player of the Year by the Vince Lombardi Committee. From day one in pro football, I never once took it for granted. It was like being on a victory tour. Each day and each game was more than a dream come true.

I've said many times that I was lucky to have played in the real NFL. I was a young pup playing with guys like Steve Nelson, John Hannah, Steve Grogan, Stanley Morgan—men who were a part of the vintage days of the NFL. I'll never forget the day I walked in the Patriots locker room and there was this veteran sitting at his locker smoking a cigarette. What? I was shocked. I'd always heard that if you smoked, you couldn't be an athlete.

Also, back then, entourages weren't a part of the rookie package. Rookies didn't show up acting like they made the league what it was. I played when you respected the game and its players.

When you were drafted by a team, you played for that team unless you were traded. Plan B free agency was just beginning when I got out of the league in 1989. The NFL is all business today. Money . . . money . . . money! It's huge today. I don't want to sound like I was broke because I was anything but. The contract I signed to enter pro football was the highest salary for any rookie to enter the game. I signed a four-year deal for $2 million. Tons of money for a guy who lived in a one-bedroom apartment while in elementary school, sharing a bed with my brother and mom. Today, my contract would have been worth $3 to $5 million dollars . . . a year!

Some say I was born too soon—not me. Thank goodness I touched and played in the original NFL.

ON TOUR

Hands down, the most enjoyable thing I've ever done in broadcasting was the spring tour trip I took around the country in 2008. Announcers never take the time during the spring preseason to visit schools—mainly because we aren't paid to do it, and furthermore, there isn't a significant programming avenue for the content you'd come up with anyway.

For me, the purpose of the tour was to go around the country during a somewhat down time to visit with coaches, players, and administrators. I wanted to strengthen already established relationships and forge new ones. It's funny; I didn't know what to expect and, I later came to find out, neither did the schools.

My standard line to each school when I called to arrange a visit was, "I'd like to come spend time with you all and watch practice. I'm on my own nickel with this tour—no ESPN producers attached."

"Really?" was the typical reaction. "Well, come on!"

Not one school refused to see me. I didn't expect rejections, since I knew almost all of them from having visited in previous years during the season, but this was an unprecedented visit for a broadcaster. As a matter of fact, it wasn't long before I started hearing from schools that I hadn't planned on seeing, wondering if I was going to make it there, as well.

What really cracked me up was that, as time went on, each school started to hear about my visits around the country. Coaches and players couldn't wait to hear what I thought of this school or that school. Every one of them wanted to know how they compared to their competition. It was hilarious, but telling. Of course, it makes sense: coaches see one another only at certain events during the year or on the football field when playing each other. Most will tell you the first thing they do during pregame warm-ups is to look at the other team's players. What do they look like in person (or on the hoof, as we sometimes say)? Game film can only show you so much.

The logistics of my preseason spring trip were challenging. I had to regionalize each week to be able to pull it off. For instance, I lumped Georgia, Auburn, and Florida together one week. Ohio St., Michigan, and Notre Dame went together, as did Texas, LSU, Oklahoma, and Texas Tech. Out west, I hit up UCLA and USC. I had to make single trips for a few, like Miami and Texas A&M, because of practice date changes. Another huge issue was transportation. The only way to pull off this jammed-up schedule and to allow for total freedom and flexibility of time with each school was to fly private.

For example, at LSU Les Miles let the assistant coaches take the night off to take me to dinner at Sammy's. We ate more crawfish than I thought humanly possible. I was having a blast shooting the breeze with these guys, and the last thing I needed hanging over my head was a flight time to catch. Other times the weather would force a team to change their practice times, so I had to be flexible. Let me tell ya—as they say, it costs a pretty penny to fly private. I wasn't doing it to be a fat cat, I promise you that. I was doing it because I was hoping to make an investment in myself and the people I do business with. The return on my investment was unbelievable, and the memories will last a lifetime.

One of the craziest and most electric places I visited was the University of Southern California, and I guess I shouldn't have been surprised. Pete Carroll had won two national championships in his first seven seasons there, and without a doubt, he has more talent on his roster than any team in the country. All that talent and competitiveness on the same field are bound to produce results—and it did for me in the first few minutes of watching them practice.

"All right, Fili! Stick that damn SC helmet decal up under his chin strap. Drive his ass to the other end of the field. I want you to pound his butt into the ground!"

USC defensive line coach David Watson was feeling the moment—screaming at the top of his lungs, veins popping out of the sides of his neck. Watson was challenging his senior defensive lineman to get the job done. The rest of the D-line joined in to create a buzz that had everybody on the field watching to see what was going to happen next.

"Give me Martin. Let's go! Get up here."

This was what it was all about on this warm spring day at the practice field on USC's Los Angeles campus: offense vs. defense; bragging rights for the rest of the practice. But more important, setting the foundation—the very basis for the war in the trenches—for the 2008 college football season.

Longtime offensive line coach "Golden" Pat Ruel knew the drill, and he had practiced it incessantly with his hulking offensive linemen. The drill was all about intensity and technique. There was a 2×12-inch, 6-foot-long Styrofoam board on the ground that the players had to straddle and not cross with their feet. The purpose was to teach players—on the offensive and defensive lines—to keep a solid base and not cross up their feet as they were blocking or charging forward. Short, choppy, driving steps were necessary to succeed in the drill and on the field. Cross up the feet and you'd be off balance—and then you'd get whipped by a 300-pound lineman.

"Martin! You ain't been beaten all spring. Kick his ass! Shut 'em up!" Ruel implored his lineman, Martin Coleman.

And there I was, standing right next to the two gladiators who were about to take part in this crazy challenge.

A small circle had formed around the two players, reminding me of a scene right out of *Mad Max beyond Thunderdome*: "Two men enter; one man leaves!"

The gathering was so tight that the intense smell of sweaty bodies brought me back twenty-plus years to my playing days, sweating and pounding through the drills at SMU. For a second, I almost wanted to jump into the circle. My knees were bent and ready to go. But then I realized that these two specimens, staring each other down and looking to take off each other's head, were a few decades younger and full of vinegar. But that's how caught up I was in the moment.

The trash talk being barked between the O-line and the D-line was heavy. And while the bystanders were going nuts, the two participants were focused and locked in—not saying a word; both thinking about their strategy. Pride was on the line.

At the clap of the coach's hands, it was on. Both players came off the ball like two massive bulls in a pasture battling for supremacy. I had yet to scout the two contestants—my upcoming season as the on-air college football analyst for ABC and ESPN was still almost four months away—but based on pure looks, I would have gone with the defensive lineman, Fili, a good-looking player, standing 6 feet 5 inches and weighing a solid 295 pounds.

But I'd have bet wrong, because Martin, a key component of USC's offensive line, kept his 325 pounds low and won the battle of leverage, exploding forward and knocking Fili off the line. Within three seconds the tilt was over. Martin remained undefeated in this drill, a hero to his O-line mates, who were all hootin' and hollerin' and talking plenty of smack to their team-mates on the opposite side of the ball.

After a few minutes the horn blew, and it was time to move on to the next drill. I was stoked to see what USC coach Pete Carroll had lined up for his boys. With goose bumps covering my body, I felt rejuvenated—like I was back on the field in my playing days. And practice was just getting under way. I couldn't wait to see the rest of this exhibition. Here are my thoughts from that visit.

APRIL 16, 2008

After my USC visit: Orderly chaos comes to mind when I try to package my thoughts on my USC visit. For example, Coach asked me to join him in his team meeting before practice started. I figured he just wanted me to listen in and learn. Well, I walked in their auditorium where the team meets and it was full of guys jackin' with each other. I kid you not. It was easily the most lively, free-spirited meeting I've ever seen. Coach Carroll walked down to the front and started whistling and telling the team to listen up. But there was this commotion going on between an offensive coach and a defensive coach—players piping in, too—about how during the previous practice the defense was getting boned with the wheel route.

"Man, y'all can't even cover a running back out of the backfield running an out and up!"

"We owned y'alls' butt! Yaaaa!"

And tons of laughter pursued. Well, Coach finally got the team to settle down, and he said that he wanted them to give me a warm welcome. Man, I was nervous as all get-out, standing in front of the most talented team in the country—and they're clapping for me. I was floating on air, with chants from lots of players imploring me to "give us some love this year."

As the season would later reveal, this team didn't need anything from me. They were going to be their usual great football team and march toward another Pac-10 title and Rose Bowl victory.

●　●　●

After visiting many of the best programs in the country, I can't tell you enough just how important the spring season is for laying the foundation for the fall. Even I had no idea going in what to expect—and I played college ball. But the game has changed so much—and there is so much pride and money at stake—that spring practice has become the time and place to separate yourself from your competitors. And as a result, what I discovered on my trip was eye-opening.

College football has an annual cleansing and evolution that takes place over fifteen practices during the spring. I was able to observe firsthand how many of the top programs in the country shape their teams. Being able to feel the football culture and the expectations of each school allowed me to better analyze each program during the season.

During this trip and throughout the entire season, I kept a detailed diary so I could relive, in my own words, exactly what I was feeling on the road. The initial goal was to help me with my research for this book, but the more I read back on this diary, the more I realized just what a useful device it could be for telling my story. So throughout this book, I'm going to use notes from my diary and my personal thoughts before road trips to allow you to have a feel for what I was thinking going into a situation. My goal is to try to have you walk in my shoes—to see what I saw and to better understand the experiences I've been through.

For instance, my first trip of the spring was to Austin, Texas, to hang out with the Longhorns. Head coach Mack Brown has always been extremely nice to me, so I knew he'd have some interesting things to say six months before the season was even going to begin.

MARCH 3, 2008

Pre-visit: I'm a little nervous . . . feels like the first school visit I made as a broadcaster. But I know Mack and the UT staff will be great hosts. I've got lunch scheduled with QB Colt McCoy, and I want to see practice. I can't wait to see if new defensive coordinator Will Muschamp is going to be a fit for UT defense. Reputation among locals is that UT is "soft."

MARCH 4, 2008

Post-visit: The University of Texas and head coach Mack Brown have the absolute best model for how to market and sell a program. The elevator door opened, and I walked in and pushed the button to go up to the coaches' offices. As soon as the door closed, the Longhorns fight song cranked up for me to listen to. The door opened to a wall full of former players who've won the Heisman trophy or have been named All Americans. The old saying that first impressions are lasting ones holds true for sure at UT!

Mack's the kind of person who wants to make visitors feel welcome, so being a good salesman is second nature to him. He's not selling, just being himself. Even though he's not from Texas, he's sure mastered the mannerisms as if he were a native.

His office was my first stop. In I walked and there he was standing with his wife, Sally. I love walking in to his office because it's the ultimate Hall of Fame room for UT sports. There are photos of former great QBs, including Vince Young, memorabilia from former UT baseball star Roger Clemens, several past presidents have stopped by for visits, and, of course, a beautiful saddle designed for Mack is next to his desk. Mack's office screams of Texas history and tradition. Any recruit, including mom and dad, who visits this office will leave with a lasting impression.

Not long into our visit, record-setting QB Colt McCoy walked in to meet me for our scheduled lunch date. Colt's a great kid who knows how to act and handle himself in any type of setting. But on this visit, Colt forgot to take his hat off when greeting Sally and me. Coach tried to elbow him with a quiet suggestion/reminder to take off his hat without embarrassing Colt. I laughed inside at the mentoring taking place.

Later on at lunch I laughed and joked with Colt about him not taking his hat off. He kind of sheepishly smiled and just said, "That's Coach Brown for ya."

Lunch was great. We had Mexican food at one of my favorite places in Austin, El Arroyos. I was able to talk with Colt about his progress and plans for the upcoming season. But before we could get into the meat of football, we both shared pictures and talked about hunting and fishing. Both of us love to get away and into the woods to relax. Coach Brown said he never has to worry about McCoy getting in trouble on the streets in Austin because he spends his off time on a lake fishing or in the woods hunting.

As for the gridiron, we really talked about spring practices and going against his own defense with new coordinator Will Muschamp in charge. Muschamp joined Texas's staff after building a solid reputation at Auburn as an attack guy. And boy does Muschamp attack! McCoy was quick to vouch for that. He said that after every practice his head is exhausted from having to focus so hard during workouts. It's blitz-ville time now at UT!

• • •

Now that I have the benefit of hindsight, it's obvious to me that all of that preseason blitzing and pressure not only helped Colt McCoy prepare for the '08 season, but it also really forced the UT offensive line to make good, quick decisions in pass protection.

All that work paid off for the 'Horns during the 2009 Fiesta Bowl as the Ohio State Buckeyes tried to blitz McCoy time and again. But it didn't work, and all that spring prep paid off in a big way as the 'Horns won with 16 seconds to go in the fourth quarter on an incredible TD pass off a blitz attempt by the Buckeyes.

And remember I wrote in my pre-visit notes about UT possibly being "soft"? Well, it didn't take long for me to realize that UT was anything but soft. After my lunch with Colt, I attended a UT practice, and I was suitably impressed.

Coach Brown was my personal escort for the practice, explaining along the way what he was looking for from each drill. Mack was also quick to point out how intense his team was at practice. I cracked up inside, thinking Mack must have been sensitive to the subject of being soft and not particularly fond of the local media who had tagged his group with that label.

I often laugh at the local media when they come out with something pretty serious in nature about football. Heck, most members of the media couldn't draw up a defensive or offensive formation, yet they are experts on football strategy? Come on!

But I digress. The point is that I was sufficiently satisfied that these Longhorns weren't going to be soft in 2008. But I wasn't convinced they were going to win the conference, either. As a matter of fact, I left Austin thinking the 'Horns would lose three games, maybe four, during the '08 season. I liked their offensive line, thought they'd be okay at running back, and knew they needed receivers to step up. During spring practices, they were strongly considering rotating another QB in with the established starter, McCoy. After all, McCoy had come off a record fresh-man season for TD passes and very few interceptions into a sophomore year where he struggled with lots of interceptions and many mistakes. So it wasn't a given that he'd be the main man his junior year.

I did like Texas on the other side of the ball, though, especially with Muschamp on board and bringing a ton of expectations and excitement to the huddle.

It turns out that I was as wrong as I could be about the '08 Longhorns. They ended up losing only one game—a heart-breaker to Texas Tech by only six points—and probably should have been playing in the National Championship game instead of Big-12 rival Oklahoma, who Texas had beaten 45–35 earlier in the year. Texas even spent three weeks as the number-1 team in the country.

What I failed to realize last spring—and what Mack Brown had no idea about during the spring, either—was that this squad was going to be a great *team*. There weren't a lot of individual stars; rather, UT consisted of a whole bunch of guys playing together. The 2008 'Horns played great all year long and were in the thick of things till the very end.

• • •

One of the funnier moments of my spring trip happened during my visit with UCLA. The Bruins are one of the teams trying to catch the mighty crosstown rival USC Trojans. Oh, the Bruins have had their moments over the last several years, but the toast of LA is definitely USC. With the arrival of new head coach Rick Neuheisel, however, UCLA was looking to stem the momentum of USC and put the Bruins back on top as the talk of Tinseltown.

It's important to realize that successful coaches are very competitive and don't want the "other guy" to have something they don't. Well, in this particular rivalry, USC has everything going for it with the media, the fans, and the Hollywood stars. Drop by any USC practice and you might see Will Ferrell, Tiger Woods, or any number of celebrities or former Heisman Trophy winners walking the sidelines and hanging out. That's a mighty powerful visual for a potential recruit. It's also tremendous motivation for the players on the field. Who wants to get shown up in front of Will Ferrell? This is what I call the "wow factor": create an environment that is to die for, and you will create a winning program. Of course, at the end of the day, nobody wins without talent, but a wow factor will help recruit and retain that talent—and being able to stockpile talent and reload year in and year out is the key to consistent success.

Which brings me back to Coach Neuheisel. I've known Rick for many years, and I am a big believer in him as a coach. One of his greatest assets is his ability to market and sell a program. Here's a coach who was a walk-on QB at UCLA and worked his way to a starting role in 1983 as a senior. But after a dismal start to the season, he was benched. That motivated him even more— Neuheisel continued to battle and was reinstated as the starter. The Bruins ended the season as Pac-10 champs. Not only that, but Neuheisel led his team to a huge upset of number-4-ranked Illinois and earned Rose Bowl MVP honors. That kind of perseverance is why Rick will be a winner at UCLA. It won't happen overnight, but in my opinion, UCLA was the downright winner during the 2007 offseason by bringing Rick back on campus as their head coach. Rick understands the ins and outs of competing in Los Angeles—for talent *and* for attention. And he's well aware that Pete Carroll sells and markets and recruits as well as anybody in America. Rick has to match the intensity of Carroll in every way or else he and UCLA will continue to play second fiddle to Carroll and the Trojans.

So during this West Coast Pac-10 spring practice tour, I had dinner plans with Rick at the Hotel Bel-Air. Talk about plush. The Hotel Bel-Air is maybe the most opulent, beautiful hotel I've ever been to. I'm just a small-town boy at heart and wasn't quite prepared for the glitz and glamour that this boutique L.A. hotel—located right across the street from the UCLA campus, of course—had to offer. Neuheisel knew all too well the affect this location would have on his guests—one of the reasons why he's a great choice to give Coach Carroll a run for his money in the Hollywood recruiting game.

I was staying at a hotel down the street and took a five-minute cab ride to get there. I was instantly overwhelmed and a little embarrassed because, as I crept up in a beat-up blue-and-gold cab, limos and Town Cars and luxury automobiles cruised on by us. Though that type of luxury isn't really my style, I began to fully understand the Hollywood concept that "Image is everything." Fortunately, I was early and nobody was milling around when my beat-up cab arrived in front of the hotel.

I waited alone, admiring the immaculate landscape of this place. It was quiet and peaceful, and I could hear the birds singing. I was lost in reverie when I noticed, out of the corner of my eye, a striking blonde turn the corner. It was Reese Witherspoon. Well, I'm here to tell you that I was absolutely starstruck. She was strolling along, singing a song, and walked right in front of me. Here was my big moment to play a part in the Hollywood scene . . . and I said nothing. I couldn't—I was speechless. The only thing going through my mind was how nice she looked and that she was great as June Carter in *Walk the Line*, for which she won an Academy Award. Now, imagine what kind of impression Reese Witherspoon would have on a potential recruit. See my point?

Rick had told me to meet him in the bar at 7:30. Bar? At this place? How could you name anything a "bar" in this place? Needless to say, the beverages seemed a little colder and a lot tastier than at the other establishments in the neighborhood.

In attendance for the dinner were Rick; former Bruins QB and fellow ABC analyst David Norrie; Terry Gannon, another ABC colleague; big-dog ESPN/ABC college football programming director Dave Brown; Ed Placey, the coordinating producer of ESPN/ABC college football; ESPN senior college football producer Bill Bonnell; and me.

I couldn't wait to tell my dinner partners about the encounter with Reese Witherspoon. Everybody at the table was envious and wished that they'd seen her, too. Well, about two hours into "cocktail hour," Witherspoon came strolling through the bar. I bumped Brown and tapped Neuheisel's leg, and they both looked up to see her pass by. She made her way out of the room, giving us the opportunity to act like a bunch of high school boys who had just seen the prom queen make a graceful exit from the cafeteria. Boys will be boys.

And then, like Clark Kent leaving a room to change into Superman, Neuheisel was in hot pursuit of Witherspoon. She had stopped briefly on her way out, and Rick took full advantage of the pause. How's this for a lame line?

"Oh, hello, Reese. I'm Rick Neuheisel, new head football coach at UCLA. Are you a college football fan?"

I'm embarrassed for Rick just by telling this story, but deep down I know he would appreciate it because we were all very impressed with his tenacity and the real reason for his pursuit.

It turned out that Witherspoon *was* a college football fan.

"Great," said Rick. "We'll have to get you on the sidelines for our opening game."

Like all good recruiters, Rick got right to the point. And since UCLA was opening the 2008 season on ESPN against national powerhouse Tennessee, what better game to showcase Witherspoon on his Bruins sidelines? Take that, USC and Pete Carroll. The Bruins can play in La La land, too.

But then came a response that even I couldn't have set up better. "Well, Coach," Witherspoon replied. "There's a slight problem with that. You see, I'm a *huge* Tennessee fan. I love Peyton Manning, and I love the Vols."

Kaboom!

With the wind out of his balloon and his superhero cape a bit wrinkled, Rick smiled politely, excused himself, and made his way back to the table.

Like I said, I'm not sure if I'm embarrassed for Rick because of his goober line to Witherspoon or highly impressed with his courage to go up to her in the first place so that he could talk up his football program, but the bottom line is that Rick is determined to create an atmosphere of excitement at UCLA—and I think he will succeed.

APRIL 18, 2008

Post-visit: Watching the Bruins practice blew me away—
but not in a good way! I bet they fumbled the QB-center
exchange fifteen times during practice. Unbelievable.
I know Rick was fuming and trying to hold it in. No doubt
he wanted to impress me and the others who were
watching that day. What impressed me was the quality of
the coaches that Rick had. Former USC and Tennessee

Titans offensive guru Norm Chow was leading the Bruins now, and the defense was led by Dewayne Walker, another highly respected coach.

There was a lot of coaching going on—not hollering like you see at some schools. Teach 'em, don't just cuss at 'em. What was missing, however, was talent. Very obvious.

I know it was early in the year, but I left that practice thinking the Bruins might win a couple of games, if they're lucky. However, the team doubled up my expectations with only four wins all year, including the season opener against SEC powerhouse Tennessee—in overtime—on national TV. It was a great way to start the season, but clearly, Neuheisel needed a season to get things together and try to succeed. The silver lining was that UCLA was very competitive in several defeats, including the season finale with bitter rival USC.

• • •

Speaking of trying to succeed, the Fighting Irish of Notre Dame have been in a slump for so long that most parents have to tell their kids that "ND" used to stand for something!

The Irish are arguably the most storied program in college football history, having won more national championships than any other school as well as having produced seven Heisman Trophy winners. But their last title was in 1988, and the Irish of late have become a bashing board for national talk-show hosts. The Irish used to dominate people with guys like Aaron Taylor up front leading the way, and a bruiser like Jerome Bettis carrying the ball. Not only has the talent been lacking, but so has that "get after you" mentality.

34

Head coach Charlie Weis was hired to bring the team back to glory. After all, Weis graduated from ND and has a genuine love for his school. But even Weis's hiring was met with tons of criticism, mainly because he was replacing an African American coach, Ty Willingham. Coach Willingham hadn't done all that bad, and it didn't help that after the first few years of service at ND, Weis's record wasn't any better than Willingham's was through the same number of games.

APRIL 2, 2008

Pre-visit: Weis doesn't care much for ESPN. A few of my colleagues rip the Irish every chance they get. If not for friend and co-defensive coordinator Jon Tenuta going to bat for me with Weis, I wouldn't have gotten the okay to visit. Weis didn't say yes until two days before my trip started. So saying I was a little anxious when I walked into the coaches' offices is a little understated.

APRIL 4, 2008

Post-visit: For those who haven't had the opportunity to see the Notre Dame campus, let me tell you it's a neat place that screams of tradition. And money, too! The buildings are beautiful—great architecture. While the Irish haven't been winning on the field, they for sure have been winning in the game of monetary donations. The football offices are second to none. And as Weis would later tell me, they have to be top shelf in order to overcome the recent lack of winning and as a way to thereby impress blue-chip recruits.

So here I am being led down a quiet hallway to meet with Charlie Weis. Dang, it was weird! I'm not much for being intimidated by anyone, but the whole atmosphere had this air of "watch what you say and do" about it.

I walked in to the coaches' meeting room, which closely resembled a corporate board room. Weis was friendly and shook my hand, and we exchanged pleasantries for a long time. But then Weis went on to explain why he was unhappy with ESPN. He said he didn't appreciate announcers going out of their way to pop the Irish. Sure, he said, we have been bad and haven't done anything to quiet the critics. He understood that. But what I was thinking while sitting there was, "Here's a coach who's got a Super Bowl ring from his days with the New England Patriots, and he doesn't like being second-guessed by folks who don't know what is really going on at his alma mater."

There's no doubt in my mind that Weis knows a lot about football. But even he probably had no idea how low the program had dropped and how much the landscape of college football had changed over the years. There are programs with student/athletes, and there are programs with athletes. Know what I mean? I've always said, show me a team with a collective high GPA, and you'll more than likely be showing me a losing team! The Irish definitely are a team with a high GPA. And there's nothing wrong with that, but fans don't want to hear that or accept that their team is too smart to compete for the Top 10.

Let me tell you: hands down, there are lots of players in college football who leave high school thinking "three and out." Meaning they intend on getting to the NFL as soon as possible. Getting an education isn't something that's very important to them. So while these stargazers are sleeping in or working a little extra in the weight room, the student/athlete is off to class or the library to get an education.

My office visit with Weis went really well. I think he realized that I was there trying to get to know him and his team so that I could truly understand them before the season and therefore be a better analyst regarding the Irish.

On the practice field the Irish impressed me. I had just left Michigan and Ohio State, so it was really fresh in my mind what two top programs' players and practices looked like. The Irish have been lacking a good-looking offensive line. By that I mean guys who look the part and fill out their pants. Their QB Jimmy Clausen showed lots of upside and a big arm; the runners were good; a couple of good receivers, too. And the defense was optimistic with the hiring of defensive guru Jon Tenuta just weeks earlier.

A personal highlight for me was being allowed to speak to the team after practice. No doubt that I was speaking to a group of student/athletes who were paying attention and who were respectful. As with most players I speak with, I encouraged them to work hard and appreciate where they are and what they have—to give all they have so that when they are finished playing, they won't look back and say to themselves, "I wish I would have done this or that." As a former player, I'm really glad that's something I don't have to say.

• • •

The next morning my phone rang, and it was head coach Charlie Weis. I was honored when Coach Weis asked me what I thought of his team and if I had any suggestions for them. I know some skeptics will say that Weis was just playing me, but I've been around long enough to know when a coach is on the up and up. Weis is smart and wanted to hear what I had to say about his team, especially how they compared to the other top programs I visited. Smart people ask questions and then listen. He might not have agreed with my assessment of his Irish squad, but at least he wanted to know what it was.

In case you're wondering, I told him just what I told his team after practice: they are talented and look good in pads, but they need to practice with a sense of urgency and passion to get better. If they do that, they have a chance to beat anybody they play during the 2008 season. I told Weis about a couple of things other schools were doing to "compete" in practice. Like at Oklahoma, where Bob Stoops grades every snap of practice with a win for the offense or the defense. At the end of practice, the losing unit has to run sprints. Bummer. Nobody wants to run after practice, and therefore guys get after it every snap.

At Georgia, Mark Richt starts practice with a "crazy man" drill. Basically, it's two-on-two or one-on-one with a ball carrier who has to stay within cones that are only ten yards apart, so contact is expected and toughness is a must. These drills and games are there to encourage competition.

As for my trip to South Bend with the Irish, I've been accused of drinking the Kool-Aid! I stood up in front of my ESPN/ABC colleagues during our August seminar and told them about my trip to ND. I was so fired up with what I thought the Irish would do that I told my brethren the Irish would win a minimum of nine or ten games.

Oops!

As we'll see, by the end of the '08 season, winning nine or ten games was a pipe dream of mine . . . and theirs!

I called Charlie throughout the season for updates and had an early December call with him for a season-ending report. Basically, Charlie told me he was going to take full responsibility for the QB and for calling plays. Weis is smart and knows '09 is it—and if he doesn't win and win early, the chances of him lasting the whole season will be slim to none. If the Hawaii Bowl victory and production from his QB is any indication of things to come, the Irish just might be back on track.

Overall, the spring tour was more than I could have ever imagined—and then the season began . . . and that's when all hell broke loose.

THURSDAY NIGHT FOOTBALL

During the summer, my time is spent hanging out with my family, getting ready for the football season's long, exhausting grind. But the summer of '08 was quite different. My internal clock/calendar was off, no doubt messed up because of the spring tour. I was cranked up to see how all these schools would emerge from their spring renewals. I remember having a conversation with my friend and ESPN college football senior coordinating producer Ed Placey, and Ed said how he couldn't wait to see how I was going to use all this new material. That made two of us.

If there was a general theme or takeaway from my spring tour, it was that there are a lot of really talented teams in college football these days. And what separates the top teams from the second-level group is the level of intensity with which the great teams practice. I kid you not, it's as simple as that. There's a reason the SEC is the best conference in America: the coaches are extremely hard and demanding on the players. Expectations to win are real, and the consequences of losing are almost unbearable.

I remember standing with the offensive linemen at Georgia, listening to offensive line coach Stacy Searles drive the dog out of his guys. There were times when I thought one of his hulking linemen was going to punch Searles in the mouth. But as the season unfolded, I watched with admiration how the Georgia O-line came together to be as good as they could be. All that hard work Searles put his unit through paid off.

After seeing twenty of the best programs in the country, I was as confident with my preseason picks as I'd ever been. I figured that having all this firsthand information and knowledge would make my preseason favorites a lock. But oh, how wrong I would be.

To me, the two best teams entering the 2008 season were USC and Ohio State. The Trojans were the best team I'd seen in the spring, and Ohio State was just behind. Both teams had talent and coaching. But there was a huge difference in the way they practiced. Remember my saying that intensity separates teams? Nobody comes close to USC in terms of intensity. Every snap is full-tilt—injuries be damned.

The Buckeyes, on the other hand, were more controlled with their routine. Coach Jim Tressel told me his challenge was to not let one of his senior stars get hurt during spring. See, Tressel appreciated the fact that two or three of his potential first-round draft picks decided to return to school for their senior seasons.

Don't get me wrong. Coach Carroll worries about his guys getting hurt, too. But USC is so loaded with talent that if he does lose somebody, there's another great player ready to step up. As for Tressel, he's got a different team with a different makeup of stars. In my opinion, no other team in college football has as many future NFL players as the Trojans. Therefore, Tressel isn't in the boat all by himself regarding safety at practice. It's a great challenge for all schools to practice with intensity while thwarting the risk of injury.

As an example, the Buckeyes had two returning seniors: All-American linebacker James Laurinaitis and defensive back Malcolm Jenkins. No doubt these two great players risked millions of dollars by coming back for their senior seasons. So I completely understand and don't blame Coach Tressel for being sensitive and caring for his players—he understands that there is a potentially lucrative professional career for these stars. Because of that, he makes sure his practices strike the right balance of safety and intensity.

APRIL 3, 2008

Post-visit: I left Ohio State totally impressed by what Tressel and his staff stand for. They compete and want to win, but care equally about their players going to class and graduating. They've got this mentoring system where each player knows he's got a person who will physically come by every class they have to make sure that player is in class. If not, the player gets a call from the mentor and receives somewhat of a demerit. If a player reaches a certain point of negatives, the mentor and player have a meeting with Tressel. Coach lets them know that if they don't get it straightened out, they'll begin to lose benefits—tickets to games to start with—and if that doesn't work, they'll lose playing time, too.

I'd just left Notre Dame the day before and was highly impressed with their facilities—same goes for the Buckeyes. It's easy to see why they win and are most any recruit's dream school come true.

So I saw an interesting contrast in styles between what I believed were the top-two preseason teams: in-your-face USC versus determined yet reserved Ohio State.

• • •

I've been a voting member of the Associated Press poll for many years and take great pride in being allowed to weigh in on such a credible panel. There are only sixty-five media members on it. Throughout *Game Day*, you'll travel with me as I fill out my ballot for the '08 season. You'll be able to see just how challenging and uncertain college football is—and how hard it is for the voters to get it right. And we don't always get it right.

My preseason ballot was due August 1, 2008. Here is how I thought the teams should start out, along with a nugget on each as to what I was expecting from them in 2008:

Preseason Ballot

1. USC: Great defense; I think Mark Sanchez at QB will be better than hoped for by Trojans fans.
2. Ohio State: A huge offensive line and stellar defense led by All-American James Laurinaitis.
3. Florida: Tough to get out of my mind what I saw in spring scrimmage, with the Gators' awesome defense flying all over the place and creating problems for the offense.
4. Oklahoma: Best QB I saw in the spring was Sam Bradford.
5. LSU: How can you not like the defending champs? But they've got to find a QB or else they've got no shot.
6. Georgia: Tough schedule, plus not being big and physical enough up front, especially offensive line, will make things tough on QB Matthew Stafford.
7. West Virginia: Even though they lost head coach Rich Rodriguez, they still have speedy QB Pat White.
8. Missouri: Most of the defense returns along with Chase Daniel and company on offense.

---

9. Clemson: Loads of talent, including a pair of running backs to die for.
10. Virginia Tech: Frank Beamer and his staff will continue their beat of greatness, but they must establish the QB position.
11. Auburn: Great-looking team with my only concern being that they have new offensive and defensive coordinators.
12. Texas Tech: They look the part but have to start believing they are a title contender.
13. Wisconsin: Big believer in Coach Bret Bielema.
14. Kansas: They lose a lot on defense but have lots of offensive power.
15. BYU: Very well coached and powerful.
16. Arizona State: Experienced QB and solid coaching staff.
17. Texas: Will receivers step up for Colt McCoy?
18. Illinois: Can they build off Rose Bowl appearance?
19. Oregon: Second year for offensive coordinator Chip Kelly.
20. Tennessee: Time to get back to business.
21. South Florida: QB Matt Grothe is a playmaker/ leader.
22. Penn State: Lots of potential with skill and good linemen.
23. Arizona: Ended with momentum and are now more experienced with offense.
24. Wake Forest: How can I not like the discipline of Jim Grobe teams?
25. Cincinnati: More powerful than people realize.

It's always fun to cast the preseason ballot because that means kickoff can't be too far behind—and that means I get to go back on the road, doing what I love best.

My first official broadcasting assignment for the season is the annual college football seminar that ESPN/ABC hosts each year around the first of August. It's the only time of the year when we—meaning anyone who has anything to do with college football at the network—all get together to glad-hand and talk business. We go over things like new production teams, new game announce team, rules changes, and strategies that management wants to implement for the production of games. The in-studio teams are there, along with directors, producers, marketing and sales reps, managers of each department, radio folks—everyone. If you are involved with college football, you're in attendance.

No doubt some of the things we talk about are boring. It drives me nuts to sit there and listen to how we're going to change the graphics' look on our packages. And it gets nerve-wrackin' when talent coach Bud Morgan gets up there and starts critiquing our work in front of the entire room. Man, when bad-boy "Honest Abe" Morgan starts calling out names, the ol' pucker-up factor comes into play. We all can use creative comments from time to time, but you never want to hear it in front of your peers.

One of the things ESPN/ABC does so well is to make us feel as if we're all in it together. My bosses don't walk around making you *know* that you work for them. Therefore, when managers share their goals and visions with us, we're more apt to genuinely listen and try to implement their wishes.

Last year, a big point was made about what we call "Time Spent Viewing." It's interesting how the networks know how long a typical fan stays tuned in to a game—over the three hours of game time, the average viewer goes in and out of the game and is actually tuned in to us for less than an hour. So if we are creative and can get that viewer to hang around for as little as three more minutes, the ratings bump would be noticeable.

Along with this information, we were informed of a goal called "Concentric Circle." Think of it as a bull's-eye. During a game, we stay traditional with the flow of the call. We announce the game as it comes to us. Let's say that's staying directly in the middle of the bull's-eye. Now, in order to keep viewers around longer, we were challenged to venture outside that center area with stories and thoughts. Maybe we could discuss the overall landscape of college football or certain coaches' moves or give a quick preview of games of interest from around the country. But the trick is to not stay out of the middle of the bull's-eye too long or else run the risk of not servicing the game. It's not as easy as it might sound. At the end of the day, the bigger the ratings, the more money we can get for our advertising time—and as the network makes more money, then hopefully we all do, too. I think that's called trickle-down economics.

But money aside, the goal from day one is to create the best possible viewing experience for the college football fan. That's why the brass take these meetings so seriously—it's no accident that we are the worldwide leader in sports. And if we all do our jobs properly, we can continue to bring the best coverage to the fans.

In all sincerity, while making that yearly trip to meet with all my ESPN/ABC buddies might seem like a pain, it pays off in the long run. Plus, the camaraderie and fellowship are great, and we get to hang out and talk football. For the most part, we've all been mentally dormant over the summer months, so this gathering wakes up the brain and gets us motivated for the new season.

One of my favorite sessions is when we all sit around with microphones and talk about teams and players to watch for.

What I find funny, and incriminating at the same time, is how we all pretty much look back at the previous season's bowl games and our final thoughts regarding that just-finished season, and pick back up on what we think will be the themes for the new season that's upon us. I was guilty for years of doing the same thing. But after my spring tour, I had a completely different mind-set at the seminar.

For example, it would have been easy to pick up where we ended the '07 season, since most experts predicted that the Georgia Bulldogs, with lots of returning talent led by surefire first-round QB Matthew Stafford, would be the preseason favorite and likely national champion for '08. I was thinking the same way, too.

However, during my spring visit with Georgia, as mentioned earlier, it was clear to me that UGA wouldn't have the ability up front on the offensive or defensive lines to win it all—especially playing in the SEC. I'll never forget leaving Georgia and going to Auburn the next morning for a seven o'clock workout. I was leaving what was supposed to be the numero uno team in the country and was expecting a drop-off in talent at Auburn. No way. I left Auburn's workout thinking that they had every bit as much talent as Georgia did. But, as we came to see during the season, talent alone doesn't get it done. Lots of luck and chemistry have to be in place or losses are sure to come.

The 2008 seminar had a little more significance for me than normal since I was going to meet my new analyst partner for our Thursday night package.

Thursday night college football has become like *Monday Night Football* for our fans. It's a huge package that has evolved since its inception in the early 1990s. As a matter of fact, Mike Patrick and I did some of the original Thursday night games. I remember us doing a Rutgers-Pitt game at the Meadowlands in 1992, back when Rutgers wasn't very good. In fact, neither team was very good, so they were each eager to agree to play on an odd night of the week, just for the TV exposure.

Mike Patrick was, and still is, one of the best in the business as a play-by-play announcer. But it was difficult for me to stay focused because not only did the game present challenges, but Mike was smoking a cigarette each series. It was as if our announcers' booth was in a heavy fog.

The game package has come a long way since those days. All of our teams playing on Thursday night are from BCS conferences, and we always have some of the biggest games of the season. USC getting upset at Oregon State last year is a great example. The vast majority of us felt that USC was unbeatable. It turns out that they pretty much were, save for that one game.

The Trojans had entered the September 25, 2008, game ranked number 1 and had everybody's respect. Our announce team had worked all week long to make sure we were prepared to show just how great the Trojans were. But we didn't lose sight of the fact that Oregon State was a worthy opponent that had beaten the Trojans the last time they met in Corvallis, Oregon.

Most of the time, I can tell if a team is truly ready to play or not. I can hear it in their voices during our meetings or see it in their eyes. And for this game, I really thought the Trojans had prepared well and were ready. As a matter of fact, I was standing in the middle of the field next to the linebackers for USC while they were warming up. Linebacker coach Ken Norton Jr. was pumping up his unit big-time—lots of swearing and getting into his players' backsides. While all of this was going on, their All-American linebacker Ray Mauluga leaned outside their tight huddle, looked over at me, and winked! It was a wink of confidence by Ray. The next time Ray winks at me before a game, I'll tell him to get his mind on his business.

Because Thursday nights have produced so many upsets, it's hard to predict anymore what an upset would be. Teams know for certain that they are on the big stage and that all of their peers are watching. Again, it's *Monday Night Football* for the college game. Everybody loves it—the only thing that's challenging is how the coaches have to make calendar adjustments for playing on Thursday night. It is awkward and out of the ordinary, but the value of playing on national TV definitely outweighs any negatives the teams have to deal with.

Oregon State turned out to be more ready to play that night than the Trojans, handing my number-1 preseason pick a 27–21 defeat. USC would run the table the rest of the season, but that one loss on our Thursday night broadcast basically cost them a chance to play for the national championship.

During the '07 season, my analyst partner on Thursday nights was Doug Flutie, but ESPN decided to reassign Flutie Flakes to the studio for '08. So the brass called me in late spring to tell me that they were going to put Jesse Palmer in the booth with me and Chris Fowler, along with Erin Andrews returning as our sideline reporter.

What did I think about that? they asked.

I was like, "Come on now! I don't know who this guy is other than he's a former 'Bachelor' on the reality TV show. Does he even know college football?"

I was half-joking and half-serious. I knew Jesse had played QB at Florida, so he had on-field experience, but I was a little bit worried that he knew nothing about being a broadcaster and that ESPN was using him because of his TV exposure from *The Bachelor*. But the brass assured me that he was a hard worker and that I'd like him. And if the big dogs think he's a good fit, then more often than not, they're usually right. So I was ready to give Jesse a fair shot.

AUGUST 7, 2008

I was really skeptical of Palmer . . . or for that matter
adding anybody to the booth. Knowing how hard a three-
man booth is made me concerned; plus, at the level we're
talking about, I couldn't think of anybody ready to join
us. The year before, outstanding analyst Todd Blackledge
filled in for Flutie to do a game with us and it wasn't a
good experience for me. Todd's awesome, but he's used
to having all the time in the world to make a point. Like I
said, a three-man booth is hard to do.

My first introduction to Jesse was at the August production seminar, and we hit it off immediately. The two of us stayed up pretty much all night visiting and drinking strong grape juice. I had so much fun I missed the first session of the meetings the next morning. Chris Fowler had worked with Jesse a little the previous season and liked him, and Jesse and Erin had gone to the University of Florida at the same time and knew each other. Jesse had dated Erin's roommate, so we were going to have to battle the Gator love all year.

As mentioned, Thursday night football on ESPN is scheduled viewing for college football fans, me included. It's also fun knowing that coaches and players are dialed in, too. Being the only game on that night allows us to set the table for the games to come during the weekend.

It's also a platform for us to go over issues and topics that are surrounding college football. It's a perfect environment to work on our "concentric circle." The four of us are so plugged in to the sport that we can handle any issue thrown our way. Who's number 1? Which coaches are doing good or bad jobs? What are the top teams in each conference? Who are the top players, and why—you name it and we hit on it.

One of the hot preseason topics was whether Charlie Weis and Notre Dame were going to win. Was Weis on the hot seat? As the season got under way, the seat started hot and stayed that way. I was thinking that the Irish would be really good, Fowler took a wait-and-see approach, and Palmer predicted eight or nine wins for the year.

Over the years, I've worked with lots of announcers. Most of them have been enjoyable and fun to work with. The one thing you're never quite sure about when forming new announce teams is whether the group will have "it."

"It," of course, involves a lot of things, including how you look together, work together, prepare together, and travel together. For our new Thursday night announcing team, the thing we have that I don't believe I've had over the years is the total package plus the fact that we all genuinely enjoy one another. That friendship is apparent on the air. You can't fake chemistry; viewers will *feel* it over the course of a season. The four of us spend lots of time together and are inclusive in everything we do. It begins with our travel plans, when we all try to land at the game site around the same time. That way, we have to rent only one car. Fowler likes to drive, and he thinks he knows how to get most anyplace. Truth be told, we've nicknamed him Magellan. The man gets lost all the time. Plus, he's so hardheaded about directions, he'll even override what our GPS is telling us. Erin gets an upset stomach every time she's put in charge of directions. Jesse and I get a huge kick out of watching her stress over them! No way she wants to mess up with "dad."

Other announce groups just don't do that. The time we spend together not only strengthens our bond, but it also allows us to shoot the breeze about our game on Thursday. By the time the game kicks off, the four of us are completely aware of both schools and, therefore, ready to support anything that happens on the field. I can't begin to tell you how many times during a game that I'll be about to say something and one of the other three will say it before I can get the words out of my mouth. It's awesome to be a part of a dialed-in team, and my hope is that it makes the game more enjoyable for you fans.

I've worked with Chris Fowler, and we've been good friends since 1991, my first year at ESPN. We worked with Lee Corso to form the original *College GameDay* team. Fowler is a pro; we call him "Commissioner," or just "Commish" for short. He's the man. After all, Chris lives and loves college football. Dating back to his days at the University of Colorado, he's always totally committed himself to being good at what he does. All of us know him as the host of *GameDay*, and he's really good at it. But a few years ago Fowler wanted to stretch out and become a play-by-play announcer, too.

Hosting a show and doing play-by-play in the booth are two different animals. The studio host has a format to follow, and the element of surprise is, hopefully, at a minimum. A game is live and full of surprises—the script is being played out in front of you. Your preparation is important, so you can say what's happened, why it happened, and, because it happened, what to expect next.

A different set of skills is required in the studio than for doing play-by-play. I've told Chris several times that he's really good at hosting *GameDay*, but that he's damn good as a play-by-play guy, too. I think he's excellent. Chris knows the game, he listens to what we're saying, and he initiates debate or summarizes our thoughts extremely well.

Jesse has jumped in with us and made a huge impact on our broadcast. His presence really completed the puzzle. Yeah, he's heavily recognized as "the Bachelor," but that's okay. He earned my respect immediately because this guy studies hard and wants to be great.

A three-man booth is difficult to do for many reasons. Probably the number-one issue you have to overcome is ego—is one guy talking more than the other two? Fowler sets up the play and its results and then lays out, giving us plenty of time to comment on the play. We might have thirty seconds to do our thing, sometimes less. Jesse and I have this rare ability to ping-pong back and forth during that thirty-second timeframe. We aren't up there saying the same thing and adding nothing new to the analysis. We're listening to each other and adding layers of thoughts on top of statements. I'm telling you, it's rare to find a partner who doesn't want to hog the air.

While we're up in the booth, Erin's down on the sidelines creating all kinds of commotion. I laugh and tell her that she's a coach's greatest pregame challenge. She's walking around on the field before the game while the players are trying to warm up, and they can't keep their minds on their business because she's a smart, attractive woman. But the coaches can't get mad at the players because they, too, are distracted.

Erin sometimes gets grief for being too sexy or flashy on the sidelines. She can't help the way she looks, and I tell her to just power on. For every negative thing said about her, there are ten good things said. Erin works very hard to be prepared and ready for a game. I trust her work and her information. Matter of fact, she's become a crutch for me during games. Many times I'll ask her to check in on something to verify a thought or a hunch. The key is that Erin immediately understands what I'm thinking. Again, by knowing each other so well, she's able to pick up real quickly on what I'm looking for. Her work on the sidelines completes our announce team like no other. We are continuously updated on things going on down there that we can't see from the booth. And if we know about it, thanks to Erin, you do too.

So that's Thursday nights, and when the game is over, my week is just halfway finished. I leave Friday mornings for New York to get ready for my work on ABC in the studio. I'm toast on

Fridays from doing the game on Thursday, but I have to gear up with energy and information for Saturday, too. One of the great things about doing the game on Thursday is that it forces me to be ready for the entire weekend. Sure, on Friday I'll make calls to check in with coaches and players about final plans for their games, but for the most part, I need Friday to travel and recover from the high of broadcasting live on Thursday night.

My partners in the ABC studio are John Saunders and Doug Flutie. John and I have been buddies and doing this a long time. We could fall out of bed and do a show. Doug, on the other hand, is new to the business and the college game, and therefore he's still adjusting to names and cultures, but he gets better and better with every broadcast. Like my game crew, the three of us enjoy one another and like working together. Doug and I played together for a year in New England, so our past has really helped us. Saunders and I joke that when the Lord made us, he used the same mold. John just happened to grow up in Canada and played hockey. I was reared in Texas and played football.

A couple of years ago, John brought his family to Texas for spring break. I've got this ranch about an hour or so west of Dallas/Fort Worth that is 3,300 acres and has eight miles of Brazos River frontage. John had been telling me that his girls, Leah and Jenna, were into riding horses. I was like, "Oh, yeah, right! Two teenage girls from New York City being cowgirls?"

And John's wife, Wanda, is hilarious. Before the trip, she told me that Big John had no interest at all in playing John Wayne and that he wanted no part of riding a horse. But his daughters, well, they were a different story.

To my pleasant surprise, the girls were actually darn good riders. About three days into the visit, I told the girls we were working cattle the next morning and that they were invited to help out. "Sure," they both said.

First thing the next morning, we saddled up and drove ninety bull calves into the working pens. For those of you who don't know what was about to take place, don't worry, John didn't either. The head cowboy at the ranch is Bary Clower. Look up the definition of "cowboy" in the dictionary and you'll see a picture of Bary: skinny legs, no butt, and a big ol' handlebar mustache.

So John went up to Bary and asked him what we were going to do. Bary said, "John, we're about to castrate these bull calves."

John, being a manly man, kind of grimaced at the thought of losing one's jewels. Then my Canadian buddy took a deep breath and asked Bary what castrating them does to 'em?

"Well, John, let me put it to ya this way: we're about to get these young calves' mind off *ass* to thinking only about eating *grass*!"

The Saunders family fell in the dirt laughing.

So how does this process work? Well, you need somebody working the hot stick, or electric prod, to get the calves up the chute, somebody to squeeze the chute, which keeps the cow from being able to move once they're in, and somebody to do the castrating. John's oldest daughter, Leah, was fired up crazy, sticking calves with the hot shot. She was all into it, while her dad, mom, and sister, Jenna, were standing back in shock. John likes to tell people now, especially any prospective dates for Leah, that they'd better be careful since Leah knows how to castrate—and actually likes doing it!

So there it is, the lay of the land and how I got prepared to meet the total uncertainty of the 2008 season. My partners and crew are all outstanding—of course, in our business, you'd better be good or you're out. There are a lot of people out there who would love to do what I do for a living, and they're ready to step in if one of us fumbles. That's why preparation and chemistry are key—and I like to think I bring both to the booth and the studio.

THE BIRTH OF COLLEGE GAMEDAY

College football popularity is at an all-time high, with records being set annually in attendance and in TV viewership. One of the key promotional programs out there is *College GameDay*. Chris Fowler, Lee Corso, and Kirk Herbstreit do a two-hour show each Saturday morning during the season that sets the table for the day. Each week the show travels the country to a game site chosen as the game of the week. School administrators and the students go nuts with excitement when they learn that their school will be hosting *GameDay*—it's that big of a deal. The locals turn out in huge numbers to raid the set—and to shout and show that their school spirit is better than any other school's in the country.

I take great pride in knowing I was a part of the original *GameDay* crew working with Chris and Lee starting in 1991 before leaving *GameDay* in 1996. There's no doubt in my mind that ESPN's support of college football helped make the sport as popular as it is today.

Fans are attracted to the passion of college football. There's no question that the intensity and desire of the college player to give his all each and every play has a bearing on the fans' appreciation—both for the individual players and for the teams. The NFL, and pro sports in general, are way too plastic and "professional" for most fans. Sure, TV ratings are higher for the NFL, but I have a strong belief that if you switched the NFL and college playing days—if the NFL went to Saturday and college went to Sundays—viewership for those specific days would stay the same, if not increase over what "the League" delivers.

Of course, that'll never happen because of the traditional slot the NFL has—but ask a fan on the street what they think about the pro game versus the college game, and the number-one response is that the fan just doesn't get where the NFL player is coming from. Sure, the NFL has lots of really outstanding citizens/ players. Yet, for the most part, there's no connection with a young man who's making millions and running around with his group- ies acting like a Hollywood star. It's a great life lesson about how having money doesn't mean you have class or are mature enough to handle the platform you are on.

The original *College GameDay* partners were Chris Fowler, Lee Corso, and me. We had a blast. Our first road show was in 1993 at Notre Dame. It went so well that ESPN decided to make it a weekly routine. When we went to ND we had no idea what to expect. Our set was inside the Ed Joyce Center, which was where the athletic department was located. The Irish were playing Florida State in a pretty hyped-up game.

Back then, we did a one-hour show. The day of the game was crazy, but the night before was just as memorable. For whatever reason, ESPN's travel department had a hotel room for us that was a pretty good ways from campus. Fowler and I wanted to stay near the stadium so we wouldn't have to drive early the next morning, since we had to be there by eight o'clock for a ten-o'clock show. A friend of ours had some friends who lived really close to campus, and they offered to let us stay at their house. Thinking about it now, this was a pretty weird setup that CF and I had agreed to. But anyway . . .

We went over to the house before dark to introduce ourselves. Great people. They were sitting at the dinner table and invited us to eat, but we said, "No thanks," since we were meeting some people at a restaurant for dinner. Then they showed us our rooms. It was a three-story house with two rooms up top. CF took one, and I took the other. We put our bags in the rooms and off we went to dinner.

Around eleven that night, we'd made our way back to our guest house and our new friends. CF went to his room, and I went to mine. Now this house was nice, but it was old and had this creepy feel to it. I'm sure we thought it was creepy because it was strange to us, but I'm telling you that it sure felt creepy and it was plenty dark up on that third floor.

I was almost asleep when Fowler knocked on my door and said, "Hey, man, there's this big-ass cat that came in my room, jumped up on my bed, and attacked me! The cat was hissin' and growling at me."

Commish Fowler was scared to death. I just laughed out loud and had to convince him to go back to bed. He did, but I could hear the dresser being pushed across the floor up next to his door so that bad-ass cat couldn't come back in on him.

The next morning at breakfast, Chris looked spent.

My, how times have changed. CF used to have to bunk with strangers on the road; now he gets to stay in five-star hotels doing *GameDay* and getting chauffeured around the city in a luxury bus with his face on the side of it.

In chapter 3 I was telling you about the chemistry announce teams need to have. Chris and I were well on our way to forming a pretty good relationship after that night in the creepy house. That first road show would be only the beginning of many great stories in the future.

Back then, the hour show was heavily scripted. We'd sit around in meetings for hours: the producers would ask us about a topic, we'd all weigh in with what we wanted to say, and the producers would put everything together. That script was followed by the control room and the three of us on the set and it might look something like the following.

"Nebraska's on a run now and why?" Chris would say to me, and I'd answer why. Then Chris would set up Lee. And back and forth this went. Not only did we heavily script the traffic, which means the order in which the comments will be made, but we'd all say pretty much what we were going to talk about.

For instance, when Fowler came to me on Nebraska, I might talk about the Blackshirts' defense. (For those who don't remember, that's what the Cornhuskers defense used to be called. They were kick-butt good and would dominate opponents. The Blackshirts have been MIA for several years now, which is a totally separate issue.) Lee then would talk about their talented offensive line. All this occurred before we went on air, so that the producer could see where everything was going. And the director had to know the traffic so he'd know which camera was next for the shot of whichever one of us was talking.

Then, once we were live, actually doing the show, we'd try to pull it off as if it were a natural flow or conversation. But it's hard to make it feel natural when things are so scripted. Well, eventually I got wise to preparing for a show and I wouldn't tell anybody in the meetings what I was going to say, so Chris and Lee wouldn't have time to figure out how to come back at me.

We had to evolve into this less restricted way of going on the air because ESPN had been doing it the old-fashioned way since the network's inception. I understand why: ESPN wanted a clean show without announcers talking over themselves or having somebody talk without a camera on them. There's a ton of orchestration between the control room and the announcers on the set. But over time, the three of us earned the trust of management that we were much better unscripted.

That approach brought out a truly live and natural show. Sure, we'd still have the traffic of Chris to Lee to me and back to Chris. But the three of us not really knowing what was coming allowed us to get into things all the time. Everybody knows that Corso's favorite line is "Not so fast, my friend!" I'll never forget the first time he said it. We were on the road, and I thought I'd nailed him with a great angle on why Tennessee was going to win. Lee fired right back at me, "Not so fast, my friend!" Lee had his No. 2 Dixon Ticonderoga pencil lifted up and in my face. We both cracked up, and a trademark phrase was born.

The thing that I believe made Lee and me so popular was that we would go back and forth with each other all the time. I'd always bust him—in a respectful way, of course—for making a crazy comment. I wouldn't just let him get away with saying something nutty. Lee was and is horrible with names. This year, for example, I was watching *GameDay*, and on one of their shows they were talking about Missouri's talented all-purpose player Jeremy Maclin. Well, Lee started talking about him and called him "Mack or Mecklin." Chris and Kirk were sitting up there holding back a huge laugh. I was watching it on TV and busted out loud. I immediately sent Chris and Kirk a text message, playfully calling out Lee. Kirk's great; he's 24/7 on the text and was right back at me with an LOL.

Another thing that was unique about Lee and me was our Thursday night picks. Back then, the three of us did the Thursday night *Weekend Kickoff* show from ESPN headquarters in Bristol, Connecticut. Part of that show was us picking the winners of the top games on Saturday. Man, I used to hate doing it because Lee and I were so competitive about who won or lost that it would ruin my Sundays when he beat me with his picks! And we both were terrible winners. I'd give him a crap-eating grin when I beat him, and he'd call me sweetheart and grin when he won. It pissed me off so bad—first of all, I couldn't stand getting beat, and second of all, it shouldn't have ruined my day. Our bantering back and forth was special, though. I mentioned earlier that you can't make announce teams special. They either have it or they don't; I'm proud to say that the three of us had it!

When I first started at ESPN, it was still a rather small campus, just a few buildings probably not even worthy of being called a campus, especially considering what it is today. Early on, it was just ESPN. Then it was on to ESPN Radio; then we launched the Deuce, or ESPN 2; then the dot-com came around; then ESPN News; and finally, it was *ESPN the Magazine*. And the company is still looking for ways to broaden the brand. Each division or piece of the network has its own desires and ways of covering college football. They all want information, and I'm one of those guys out on the road gathering information that is desirable. At least, it had better be. The trick is to balance how I transfer that information to each medium without going bonkers.

For example, during the middle of the 2008 season, the Oklahoma Sooners defense was giving up a lot of yards and points. Most members of the media were ripping Bob Stoops and his defense. So I called Bob, and we had a long conversation about his defense. Stoops explained to me that he was confident in his unit and that the problems weren't being made because of a lack of talent—but rather because the opponents' QBs were able to extend plays by avoiding sacks, which put pressure on his defensive backs to cover longer than normal. So Bob was working with his defensive front to make sure they didn't lose containment and kept the QB in the pocket. Bob was straightforward in mentioning that his defense was on the field more because his offense was so good and scored most of the time within six plays!

So now here I was with this in-depth conversation with Stoops. I had credible information to go along with my observations. Most all the other media members were out there throwing mud against the wall—hoping they were getting it right.

Depending on the show I was doing for ESPN, I used that material starting with Thursday night's game. In that format, I had lots more time to fully reveal my conversation with Stoops. Of course, *SportsCenter* wanted to hear about it, too, and I'd use it there. But it had to be a much more compact presentation. Then on Saturdays for the ABC studio show, I'd get into it again. At the end of the day, the key is being able to deliver the material I've gained in a variety of formats so the college football fan is getting quality material. I need to be able to wrap that information up in a thirty-second response, or extend it if the show has the time for it.

My first introduction to Bristol, Connecticut, and ESPN dated back to my playing days in the NFL. I'll never forget the week I received a call from Chris Berman asking if I'd consider driving down to Bristol and ESPN to be a part of his NFL weekly show. I was playing for the New England Patriots—around 1987—and we had an open Sunday, so Berman asked me to join him. I'd hit it off with Chris during training camp that summer and figured why not. So I followed the directions to this place called ESPN.

The place stuck out like a sore thumb. It stuck out because on the side of the road were several satellite dishes outside of a couple of buildings. I was wondering why in the world I drove three hours to do this. I'd been around TV since my high school days. I was always a spokesperson for my teams and had plenty of experience, but my involvement with TV was always in interviews—I was asked questions and then I'd answer them. That's completely different than being in a studio and having to originate ideas or comments. Berman's show was an early version of *NFL Prime-Time*. I was playing the "Tom Jackson" character early on!

Chris and I did his show from a small studio that wouldn't serve as a coat closet at the worldwide leader in sports today. It was fun, though, and afterward Chris treated me to dinner.

We had three options: McDonald's, Friendly's, or this family-owned restaurant called the White Birch that was inside a house. We chose the White Birch. I couldn't help but think, there ain't no way ESPN is going to be around for too long. Boy, was I wrong.

My first years working at ESPN were awesome. Chris Fowler, Lee Corso, Tim Brando, and Mike Tirico were basically the Bristol studio presence for college football. The staff of producers, directors, research department (which back then was maybe two guys), makeup, even the upper management was just a small group. We bumped into one another all the time. Oh, there was one other spot we could've eaten at —the cafeteria on the ground floor of the building, a one-horse stall at best. But we all hung out there and grabbed something to eat before our shows.

As ESPN started to grow, so did our wardrobe. But it took some strategic thinking to bring about change. At first, the rule for all talent was to wear a jacket some shade of dark blue. I'll never forget showing up one day with a bright blue jacket. It was one of my all-time favorites. Man, my boss looked at me and said, "What in the heck do you have on?"

I said, "Look, it's a blue jacket."

Since we didn't have any other options for me to go to, they let it slide. And once the crack in the door was there, other talent saw daylight and all kinds of colors started showing up. I take pride in knowing that I had a part in changing the culture at ESPN. And it certainly did change. That was probably in 1992, and by 1993 the cat was out of the bag. The Deuce was launched in 1992, and anything but "pilot blue" was allowed to be worn.

The Deuce studio set was in a garage in the parking lot. We froze our butts off during the winter. But I would do a 7:30 P.M. college football scoreboard show in the main building on ESPN, jump off the set, and run through the parking lot to make an appearance on ESPN 2 to do their young hip-hop version of our college football scoreboard show. ESPN 2's goal was to offer more programming to a much younger viewer.

The hosts were Keith Olbermann and Suzy Kolber. One of the segments I did was with "Hammerin'" Hank Goldberg.

I enjoyed working with all three of these announcers. It's a small world. Suzy and I had a previous working relationship from our days with the Dallas Cowboys' Silver Star Network, Jerry Jones's internal TV production team. Suzy was a producer at the time; she wasn't on the air. We had a ton of fun. It was my first TV gig, as Jerry's cohost on his weekly show. Working for Jerry was awesome. He was notoriously late, and our crew would sit around wondering what in the heck he was doing. We'd be fired-up mad at him for making us wait for hours sometimes. But as soon as he'd walk in the door, his personality would kick in and he'd have us laughing and having fun.

One time while we were waiting, I'd told the crew that when we started taping his first segment to hang in there because I was going to try to pull one over on him. I started out with my standard "Hello. Welcome to *Special Edition*; I'm Craig James along with our host, Jerry Jones." I went on to face Jerry and said, "Jerry, before we get going today on the Cowboys, I wanted to pass along a hello from an old friend of yours from back in Arkansas."

Jerry said, "Oh, yeah? Good."

"Her name is Betty . . . and Jerry, she said you were hands-down the best drive-in movie theater date in the world."

Now, I'm jackin' with him about this and making up the story, but Jerry didn't miss a beat. He said, "*Creg* . . . [he had a hard time saying "Craig"], absolutely. Betty is one-hundred-percent right. Hands down I was the best!"

I'm telling you, we all hit the floor howlin'. Jerry was as smooth and quick on his feet as anybody out there. He slapped me on the shoulder and said, "You can try me again some other day, young man." What a treat it was to work with Jerry Jones, and what a special man he is.

The first time I met Jerry was in the late 1980s, just as he was about to buy the Dallas Cowboys. We were at a black-tie fund-raiser event called the Cattle Baron's Ball. Jerry, along with his wife Gene, came up to me and introduced themselves. I was absolutely thrilled that Jerry knew who I was. Of course, I shouldn't have been surprised, because Jerry had been a football player at Arkansas, so he followed the old Southwest Conference and the days when SMU would play his Hogs. No doubt my playing days at SMU and Jerry knowing me helped me get the TV job.

The Silver Star Network was responsible for producing the Cowboys' preseason games; head coach Jimmy Johnson's weekly show; Jerry's show, which was called *Special Edition with Jerry Jones*; as well as any other programs the Cowboys needed producing. It was a great gig to learn at; being able to see how shows were put together helped me tremendously in the long run.

We taped *Special Edition* each week and always traveled to different cities around the country to tape a few segments with celebrities. The guest appearances were made by former players and actors or even singers like the Gatlin Boys. As a matter of fact, I was discovered by ESPN because one of our celebrity guests, former Dallas Cowboys player Preston Pearson, had sent a copy of the show he was on to Bristol trying to land a gig for himself. ESPN watched the tape, saw me hosting it, and liked what they saw. I'll never forget getting a call asking if I'd be interested in auditioning for a job in college football with ESPN. I said, "Heck, yes!" And the rest is history as they say. At that time, ESPN was growing and had big plans for college football. My guess is that even ESPN had no idea at that time how big and popular the sport would become for the network.

Another great moment for me with *Special Edition* was when we traveled to California to see actor Gary Busey. Gary had this awesome house in Malibu that looked out over the ocean. Well, Suzy has this tattoo on her ankle, and it was driving Gary nuts! Not that it takes much to do that, but Gary was seriously hitting on Suzy, so our crew had to play "run blocker" for her. Suzy's engaging and sweet personality was apparent then, and over the years, her personality has proved to serve her well as a top-flight on-air talent.

Back to the rest of that ESPN 2 crew . . .

Keith, well, he was different. But that's what made him so good. Keith Olbermann wasn't the average run-of-the-mill sportscaster host. He just looked at things differently, which brought about many random angles to games or to players. I loved his style.

Hank Goldberg was hilarious, and the things we were allowed to do were ridiculous. I had to change out of my coat and tie and put on a silk 1970s-style shirt before going on the air. This apparently matched the style and the look of the viewers' demographics for ESPN 2, as opposed to the blue-blazer look on ESPN. Hammerin' Hank used to bring a meat cleaver on the set with him to pound the desk with. One time I taped my fingers up as if Hank had smoked me with the hammer.

It was okay to be wacky on the Deuce, and I actually preferred it to the standard stuff we were doing on ESPN. At the end of the day, I suppose I got the call to do the Deuce because Corso didn't quite fit the demographics they were looking for—you know, the young, hip sports fan. And since Corso was a fossil, he didn't fit the bill. Just kidding. Truth be told, Corso really didn't want the gig. It wasn't his style, and the added workload wasn't something he was looking for. Plus, truth be known, most of us didn't really desire work on the Deuce. I mean, come on! It was only in a few million homes—not megamillions like big brother ESPN.

I'd finish my stint in the garage with the Deuce, change back into my blue jacket, and run over to the main building to finish the night with the "regular guys on ESPN." I look back on it now and have great memories. When I see Suzy or Keith or Hank we laugh about our gig with the Deuce and how wrong we were about the chances of ESPN 2! It's not called the Deuce anymore and is in almost as many homes as ESPN.

On the road doing *GameDay* was a blast, too. Several trips stand out to me. Here are some of my favorites:

Penn State, 1994

Penn State was playing at Michigan. The Wolverines' head coach was Gary Moeller and one of his assistants was Lloyd Carr, who'd take over the next year as head coach. Not only was Carr on that staff, but so was future Oklahoma State and LSU head coach Les Miles. Our *GameDay* trip that week was to the Big House! I'd never seen a game there and was fired up.

One of our jobs during the week back then was to go on the road and do a feature story; basically, we were the reporters. A few weeks earlier, prior to our Michigan trip, I'd been assigned to go to Michigan and do a story on running back Tim Biakabutuka, who was young and who I thought had a bright future ahead of him. Well, apparently our *GameDay* producer sold Michigan on the idea of my coming to do a story on the *entire group* of running backs instead of just Biakabutuka. We had wanted to do a feature on this talented but relatively unheard-of running back, but the Michigan program wanted us to look at the whole group.

So I made the trip, and on that particular Saturday we aired the feature, which focused on Biakabutuka. The story probably ran two weeks before our *GameDay* visit to Michigan. We always arrived at the site on Friday to prep for the show. We'd gotten there early and so CF and I decided to walk around campus. Michigan was having a pep rally that afternoon at one of the fraternity houses, so we made our way over there. I remember it like it was yesterday.

Chris and I had gone into the frat house and had just gone upstairs so we could look out a window at the pep rally below. In the hallway we ran into head coach Gary Moeller, who'd apparently just spoken to the crowd from above. Moeller saw me and came right at me, pissed as all get-out. I'm telling you, he was in my face and ready to fight. I thought it was on!

Apparently Moeller was mad at me about the feature I'd done on Biakabutuka and how I'd not really focused on the other runners. Plus, when I tagged the feature live, I gave a general comment about the practice session I'd seen as they were getting ready to play Notre Dame. I said they didn't look focused and that Moeller was having to rip 'em all the time. Moeller didn't like that observation at all. Most coaches don't; they never like anyone—especially the media—to ever question their team. So I had two strikes against me and was waiting for the third strike to be a literal one—a punch from the head coach!

Fowler got in between us and broke it up, thank goodness. Can you imagine the publicity out of that if the two of us had actually gotten into a fight? As I look back on it, it was nothing more than a breakdown in communication between us, the media relations department at Michigan, and Moeller. If Moeller had known we were featuring Biakabutuka, he might not have allowed us to see them. Or maybe he would have, but at least he would have not been surprised. At any rate, Moeller was immature with his reaction and a jerk, in my opinion. He was fired the next year and replaced with Lloyd Carr. I haven't seen the man since that day in the hallway; don't care to, either!

Needless to say, Fowler and I were a little jacked up after that, but we still went on to enjoy the pep rally.

But the real fun wasn't over; it was just beginning!

After the pep rally, Chris and I went downstairs, and just behind this frat house was a basketball court. We started shooting hoops with some guys, and the next thing you know, these two frat guys called us out to a pickup game against them. There was no way we could turn down the challenge. I had my cowboy boots on and had to borrow sneakers from somebody; so did Chris. The winner was the first team to ten points (by ones), you had to win by two points, and it was "Make it, take it."

CF and I started out ballin' like we were former hoops stars. It was 8–0 and we were talking plenty of crap. The crowd from the pep rally had stuck around, so we had a *huge* audience. The two frat guys we were playing were taller than us and no doubt had hoops in their background. They woke up. Man, it was on!

They came roaring back and tied us up. We were competing our butts off. I made a pass to Fowler, and he went up for what was going to be an easy layup. Not so fast! CF was stuffed deluxe! They tied us up at 10, and it kept going back and forth. We hung on to win 20–18. We were full-on drenched with sweat and had a roaring crowd cheering us on. Too bad YouTube wasn't around for that interesting pep rally.

Nebraska Cornhuskers, 1994

Two things stick out on this particular visit to Lincoln, Nebraska.

Before we left, Fowler and I had to go our separate ways to do features on Wisconsin and Colorado. The Badgers were playing at Colorado; both were good, and we wanted to talk about the game on our Saturday show. Fowler was covering the Buffs, his alma mater, and I was with the Badgers. We were both asked by the head coaches to speak to their teams. I gave UW a win-one-for-the-Gipper speech. I had 'em fired up and ready to play. Head coach Barry Alvarez thanked me, and I said, "No problem."

Meanwhile, Fowler did the same for CU and loved having a chance to speak to his alma mater's team.

Fast-forward a couple of days to the actual game. CU beat the snot out of the Badgers. That Saturday, as I mentioned, Chris and I were in Lincoln for a *GameDay* show and had gone out for a few beverages after our broadcast. About three in the morning my room phone rings—and there was a slurred voice on the other end asking, "Howz u like 'em now?"

I hung up on the caller, thinking it was some drunk who was playing a prank or had the wrong number. Then I realized it was Fowler having fun and rubbing it in a little bit. For the record, Coach Alvarez has never invited me back to talk to his team.

The second reason I mention this road trip is that it was the first time my kids had watched and noticed at the end of the show during our picks' segment that Lee and I put on Corn-huskers hats. They were tall rubber hats that looked like corn; we both looked like goobers for sure. I got home on Sunday and my kids said that I'd embarrassed them.

Miami and Alabama, 1993 Sugar Bowl

Chris, Lee, and I were doing the Sugar Bowl, and while in New Orleans for the week, we decided to have a little fun on Bourbon Street. Corso had more energy than Fowler and me combined. Lee's nickname is the little scooter, and he was on a roll and suggested we hit up this bar called the Dungeon. This place was nothing short of a major fire hazard. We were shoulder to shoulder with people. It was crazy—it even had a big birdcage hanging up in the corner of one room. Inside the cage was a lady who was scarcely dressed, and she was dancing.

Well, after a while, Chris and I started looking for Lee. We were a little concerned for our little buddy. Not so fast! Our concerns for Lee were unfounded; we looked up under the birdcage and saw Lee dancing with a bunch of fans. It was totally innocent, but hilarious when you think about Lee holding court in the middle of the night. Again, no way we'd get away with things like that today with YouTube and all. But it was good clean fun and allowed us to create a friendship that showed on the air.

Orange Bowl, 1992

On New Year's Eve we were doing our pre-night report from the old Orange Bowl when all of a sudden we heard gun shots and bullets ricocheting off the stadium seats. Needless to say, we had to get down and out of that stadium pronto. Crazy how this incident didn't even make the news! The locals told us it was just part of what happens in that area on New Year's Eve.

Home Game/Bristol, 1994

From time to time we'd stay in Bristol and not go to a site. We called it a "home game." Chris, Lee, and I were doing a 7:30 scoreboard show, and I was sitting there listening to CF do a highlight for a game. Well, Lee was sitting between Chris and me and listening, too. But Lee was listening to two people talk: Chris, who was doing the show, and the producer, who was in Lee's ear telling him to move his hand. Lee had this red dot painted on the desk as a reminder of where to put his hands during the shows. Lee had to be careful not to let his hand slide toward Chris or his hand would be in CF's single TV shot. Well, Dan Steir, the producer, kept telling Lee in his earpiece, "Move your hand, move your hand!" over and over again.

Finally, while semi-paying attention to Chris, I heard Lee say out loud, "F—k you!"

Chris and I both looked immediately at Lee, who was sitting there stoically as if nothing had happened. Lee was telling the producer to bug off, buddy! Can you imagine if TiVo were available then? That kind of stuff cracks me up.

Okay, so bring it full circle to 2008, and you can't even get in the ESPN parking lot without being frisked now. It's amazing how big the Bristol campus is—tons of buildings and all kinds of people doing all kinds of jobs. And for me, a huge eater, the new cafeteria is off-the-charts nice. There are different "themes" to choose from—certainly a long ways from the vending machine and small cafeteria of the early 1990s.

When I go to Bristol now, I need somebody to help me get around from building to building. Even the way our makeup is applied has changed. We used to have it put on the old-fashioned way—rubbed. Now, it's airbrushed on. Fancy stuff for a guy who grew up riding pastures and tractors. My grandfathers would raise an eyebrow at my git-ups!

As for *GameDay*, it truly has come a long way. The show's two-hour format allows Chris, Lee, and Kirk to cover just about anything going on in college football. And no, they don't have to stay at strangers' houses anymore, either. Of course, Chris and I talk about that all the time and how much fun we had. Fans ask me why I left *GameDay*. It's a very simple answer. At that time in my life, I had four kids at a very young age and they needed me to be at home more often. I was doing so much work that my only days home were half of Tuesday and all of Wednesday.

Then CBS came along and offered me more money to work only on Saturdays in New York, which was a no-brainer at that time. Still, it wasn't an easy decision for me to leave ESPN, because I loved what I was doing. But things have worked out nicely for all involved. It's funny how things come full circle—after being gone just a few short years, I'm loving my time back with the ESPN/ABC gang even more.

My time with CBS was great, too. Being able to work with Jim Nantz in both college and NFL football was a blessing. Jim is one of the best hosts in the history of announcing. His knowledge, passion, delivery, and compassion for people are outstanding. CBS did a heck of a job with their rights to the SEC games. The production of games was excellent. But unlike ESPN, CBS didn't have games from all the other conferences. At ESPN, the network is trusted in college football because fans see our announcers all over the place. From coast to coast, ESPN is on it.

I was glad for the opportunity at CBS, but am really glad to have made my way back to ESPN. Kind of a funny sidebar to this CBS talk: I'm laughing to myself at how while I'm writing this book, I am happy to be at ESPN and can't imagine going anywhere else. But the one thing that I've found in this business is that change is inevitable, so I'd better be nice to everybody and careful with what I say!

5

IT TAKES
A COACH

It used to be that a coach's job was to win games. In order to do that, he had to recruit well and coach his team to victory. But, boy, have the job descriptions and responsibilities changed over the last several years. Coaches now have to be able to recruit and coach players, market the program, glad-hand boosters, mentor the players, discipline the team, know the rules of the NCAA, make sure the players are going to classes and graduating . . . and still maintain lives of their own.

Successful coaches come in all shapes and sizes and with different styles, but all possess at least one common characteristic: a serious drive to win.

University of Texas head coach Mack Brown and Ohio State head coach Jim Tressel are two peas in a pod. They are both buttoned-up and always selling their programs to anyone who will listen. Then there are others like South Florida coach Jim Leavitt, who could not care less about the "outside stuff." Leavitt wants to coach 'em up and that's it. Realistically, he understands he has to deal with the other stuff, but it's not something he wakes every day looking forward to.

Here's what I mean: I've stood at midfield before games with both Brown and Tressel. Their teams are on the field warming up and getting ready to go. But Mack and Jim are at ease and making the rounds, saying hello to all the "big-timers" who might be at the game. The sidelines of games always have high-powered boosters milling about. Mack and Jim make sure they spend time with each one. Now I'm sure both are wired inside and anxious to get the game under way, but they appear to be relaxed and enjoying the moment.

On the other hand, Leavitt is anything but jovial and entertaining. Oh, over the years he's become a heck of a lot better with the glad-handing, and he loves his school for sure. But I remember a game where South Florida was playing as the number-2 team in the country at Rutgers on a Thursday night in 2007. I got to the stadium about two hours before kickoff. In addition to my analyst work, I've also got several responsibilities with ESPN for *SportsCenter, Pardon the Interruption*, and ESPN News that have to be taken care of. After I do that business, I like to make my way down to the field to say hello to the coaches and to get some last-minute information about the game. It never fails: coaches will spill the beans/game plan to me in sixty seconds during pregame. We can spend hours on the phone and in person during the week trying to get to the bottom line with coaches, but usually to no avail. But when I'm by myself and there are no producers or directors or strangers present, they talk quickly and freely.

Erin Andrews and I work the pregame field hard. The two of us always come away with material that either supports a thought or enlightens us to something we didn't know about.

For example, before the 2007 Alamo Bowl game I was leaving the field to get back to the booth for the kickoff. I happened to be in line with the Texas A&M coaching staff and joined them in the elevator ride up to the press box. Well, sure enough, the offensive coordinator was one of the coaches in the elevator, and I asked him if there was anything special for me to watch for. Coach Les Koenig Jr. opened right up and said, "Craig, we're going to use the lonesome polecat formation tonight to confuse Penn State. When we do it, we'll be trying to get blocking angles on the defense while they are confused and moving around."

Now, the lonesome polecat is a formation that looks like anything but a formation. You might have a center and one guard to the QB's right and then everybody else lined up wide to the outside. Coaches will tell you that it's a great way to put pressure on the defense to defend the entire width of the field. For me (and as shown by what happened in this game), it creates a lot of doubt and confusion for the defense. As soon as the offense breaks the huddle and lines up, you can see the defense running around trying to line up correctly.

Sure enough, in the second quarter, the Aggies went to the line of scrimmage in the polecat formation, just as Koenig had told me. At the snap, they handed off to Michael Goodson, who went the distance for a touchdown. The strategy of creating doubt and confusion at the snap went just as planned by the Aggies coaches. Penn State was unsure of how to line up, and it resulted in a touchdown run by Goodson. From the booth, I announced that the Aggies just ran a play from a special formation. Fowler looked at me and gave me a nod of "nice job." I went on to explain what had just happened, allowing the viewer to fully appreciate it.

My takeaway from that experience was that I was smart enough to prod a coach on a sixty-second elevator ride. One of my ESPN bosses, Jed Drake, says "Chance favors the prepared mind." Great statement and right on target. I couldn't agree more.

There have been many former players who had the looks and charisma to go on TV after their playing days were over who didn't make it. One big reason is that in order to be good year in and year out, you've got to work at it. My partner Doug Flutie is a prime example of this. Doug saw after his first year that in order for him to be good and respected as an analyst, he'd have to work harder. Being Mr. Hail Mary was a good start, but it wasn't going to keep him on TV. He needed to do more. That meant literally living the sport. It means staying current on a daily basis so that if something happens, you know how to respond. Doug had an outstanding playing career because he figured out how to prepare to be successful. Flutie knew each day of the week what he had to do. Being a football player was second nature to him. Same thing goes for being a good analyst. I respect Doug for recognizing this requirement and stepping up to the task.

In this business of being an analyst, it's imperative for me to be able to call on coaches for information. I've never considered myself to be a "newsbreaker." Guys like ESPN's Chris Mortenson or Fox's Jay Glazer are great at breaking news stories. If one of those two says something, I have confidence they aren't just winging it. It's not my style or desire to be a scoop hound, so coaches know they can talk to me about the game. Plus, I've been burned in the past trying to be a newsbreaker.

Back in the late 1990s I was doing some research for my studio work and was having a conversation with one of my go-to guys, a person whom I respect a lot and has tons of knowledge about football—not necessarily football strategy, but front-office stuff, like knowing where coaches are going and coming from. Well, he told me that then Georgia Bulldogs coach Jim Donnan was going to leave UGA and become the head coach at Oklahoma. I was like, "Wow, now that will be a big deal."

It made sense, too. Donnan coached in the '80s at OU under Barry Switzer, so he knew the turf well. I created a firestorm from the administration at UGA when I talked about the "news." They were furious—not at me but at Donnan! Obviously, they wanted to know if it was true. The fury of UGA administrators paled in comparison to the heat Donnan unleashed on me. I was reading in the paper that he was going to "sue Craig James" for slander.

I didn't know Donnan. Oh, I'm sure I'd met him, but I didn't have a relationship with him. I didn't care that he was pissed at me; I was only concerned with my source and wanted to make sure I wasn't slinging mud against the wall. I hate reporters who do that, and there are a bunch of 'em out there. They'll say something cute or smart just to get a little publicity. The Donnan move to OU never happened. I called my source time and again to verify what he'd told me. I never found out what happened. My guess at the time was that the deal was indeed in the works but that this announcement exposed the potential and therefore ended up killing the deal.

We've all heard the saying that it's a small world we live in, right? Well, about five or six years later I became a colleague of Donnan's when he signed on to work with us at ESPN. I'll never forget the first day of our August seminar when we all came together for our annual kickoff meetings. I saw Donnan in the room and felt really uncomfortable. I had no idea what he'd say or do. Then came that moment of timing and truth when we were passing by and had to acknowledge each other. I said, "Hello, Coach."

Donnan was the ultimate pro and gentleman, and he said hello back to me. We sat there and visited about college football and not once did he bring up the time when I broke the story of him leaving for OU. I darn sure wasn't going to bring it up—not during this first meeting. Well, over the years, Jim and I would visit and would always have a friendly conversation. As a matter of fact, Coach ended up having his own radio show out of Atlanta and would call me pretty regularly to join him as a guest. I've said yes to each one of his requests.

The first time I was called in to be on with him, he asked me at some point about this particular coach who was rumored to be going somewhere. I said, "Coach, as you well know, I was an idiot a few years ago and said that some Georgia coach named Jim Donnan was leaving for OU."

He cracked up and again took the high road with me and we laughed it off.

Since that Donnan experience, and over the years, I've had tons of knowledge and information about things going to happen before anybody else knew about them. And I'm not going to say I'll never break news again, but I'm always mindful of what the upside of it is for me. I'm not a rookie in the business trying to make a name, nor do I care if my name is in print. What I do with the information, though, is to dig deeper and use it so that my overall coverage of the game is higher because of what I know from a big-picture standpoint. Even if Donnan had left for OU, I'd have won the battle but lost the war. Donnan wouldn't have given me the time of day if I needed something from him—and I depend on coaches for good information.

At the end of the 2007 season, Kirk Herbstreit broke the story that his sources told him LSU coach Les Miles was going to return to his alma mater, Michigan, as their head coach. I don't know if you remember this, but it fired up Miles, who said it was false. I didn't call Kirk on it, but I sure felt for him. Kirk's excellent at what he does, and I'm sure that he, too, had more than credible support for his findings. But Miles, like Donnan, denied anything to do with it and stayed at LSU. I'm sure Miles was unhappy with Kirk for putting him through the wringer with the announcement. It's that same old scenario: win the battle but lose the war. Kirk is established and didn't need any more credibility. My bet is that Kirk is like me now on this matter and won't be breaking news stories like this anytime soon.

I'm telling you these stories because I rely on coaches. It's important for me to never forget that without total access to coaches, I wouldn't be able to perform at the level I want to be at. It takes years to build confidence with a coach, and it can be easily torn down in seconds.

Well, back to the South Florida–Rutgers Thursday night game. I was on the field and had visited with Rutgers head coach

Greg Schiano. He was very pleasant, but at the same time not exactly ready to sip a glass of tea with me, either. So I started looking around for Coach Leavitt—and the dude was running sprints on the field to try to loosen up. No kidding. He had on his street clothes and was running from sideline to sideline. And he was sweating big-time. I had to literally jump in his way to get him to stop and speak with me for a few minutes. Not even Erin's presence on the field caught his attention. He was short and to the point. Leavitt realized he needed to be polite, but it just wasn't happening. He had so much energy that he needed to work out.

So while Brown and Tressel are relaxed and have their style, Leavitt's successful with his own set ways. They call it apples and oranges for a reason.

I had three different coaches during my college and pro career. Ron Meyer was my coach for three years at SMU and my rookie year with the Patriots. Ron was a great motivator and knew how to recognize talent. Ron was like Mack Brown and Jim Tressel—he'd easily stroll the sidelines during pregame glad-handing it. Shoot, pregame was Coach Meyer's favorite part of game day! Ron loved the glitz and glamour of the game—the bands, the cheerleaders, and knowing his team was on center stage for the day.

Meyer was the first person I ever heard mention the Five P's philosophy: Proper Preparation Prevents Poor Performance. He used to say that all the time to us. It stuck with me, as I'm sure it did with many of my teammates. Coach had a vision of what a top program was supposed to look like. He'd been a scout for the Dallas Cowboys in his early days, and I'm sure that had an impact on him. How could it not have been a positive influence? The Dallas Cowboys were the model for all to follow. Tom Landry was the epitome of what a successful coach looked and acted like. Landry might not have said the Five P's, but rest assured he was 100 percent prepared as was his team on game day.

In addition to seeing Landry in action every day, Meyer also had a chance to see how the front office was run. Gil Brandt was the architect behind the powerhouse Cowboys regime. Gil found the players, and Landry coached 'em up. So Meyer took a little from both, and I'm confident that was a solid reason he was able to become a winning coach.

My senior year at SMU, Bobby Collins—a Southern gentleman who was polite and capable of shaking hands with the big dogs, but who was far more interested in getting his team ready to play the game—was our head coach. I'll never forget the day SMU announced they were hiring Coach Collins to replace Meyer, who'd gone on to be head coach of the New England Patriots. My teammates and I had just won the Southwest Conference championship in 1981. The news of the hiring came just after the season ended and we were told of Collins and his staff coming over from Southern Mississippi. We were all like, "Who in the heck is Collins, and where is Southern Mississippi?" We were obviously a directionally challenged team!

So we were talking among ourselves and concerned about these country bumpkins driving pickup trucks and chewin' tobacco who were about to coach us—the SWC champs! What could they bring to the team that we didn't already have? Man, we were full of ourselves. Looking back on it now, Collins and his staff were a great hire. Because of our previous success as a team, we needed the change that took place. Not that Meyer's staff wouldn't have gotten it done, but Collins came in and all preconceived notions about players and ability were thrown out the window. We were all starting over again and it was time to compete.

Collins and his staff knew football. Yes, some of 'em chewed tobacco and spoke in slow, deliberate drawls that made us Texans sound like we were talking at warp speed. But these coaches were Southern gentlemen who liked their football.

Ultimately, this new staff did their jobs well, as we went on to win another SWC title as well as a victory in the 1983 Cotton Bowl over Dan Marino and his Pittsburgh Panthers. Our 11–1 record was good enough for a final ranking of number 2 in the country.

And then I had Raymond Berry with the Patriots after Meyer was fired and went on to become the head coach of the Indianapolis Colts. Long story short on Meyer being fired by the Patriots: It was my rookie year of 1984, and we were a darn good team that had a 5–3 record at the midway point of the season. Ron felt he needed to make a change with the defensive coordinator, so he fired Rod Rust and replaced him right in the middle of the season. The problem was that he fired Rust while the Pats' owner, Billy Sullivan, and his son, the general manager, were out of town.

Well, a day or two later they got back in town, fired Meyer, and rehired Rust. That opened the door for Berry to become the head coach.

Coach Berry was an NFL Hall of Fame receiver who was an intense overachiever. Berry made sure we were as prepared as we could be. Coach Berry was so single-minded that I remember the time we were playing the Los Angeles Raiders in the second round of the playoffs. We traveled to L.A. on New Year's Eve. When the team was getting off the bus at the hotel, Berry announced that we had a midnight curfew. Well, we'd traveled out west a week early in anticipation of the game, and it was New Year's Eve and everyone expected we'd have a little personal time on this holiday. So several of the older veterans immediately spoke up and asked Coach if we could extend curfew just a few hours. Berry looked at the players and asked them, "Why?"

"What do you mean 'why,' Coach? It's New Year's Eve!" they replied.

Berry had no idea that it was New Year's Eve. That's how focused he was. The man was so focused on our game that he didn't have a clue what day of the year it was.

I've got all these names of coaches and the different styles each possesses; trying to figure out how to present them is next to impossible. So I thought I'd draw up what I think is the perfect coach, using examples of men who do their jobs and do them well.

First and foremost, at least in my mind, the ideal coach has to be able to recruit. If you don't have players, I don't care how good a teacher or leader or motivator you are, you aren't going to win, particularly nowadays when it's so obvious in a game if your guys can't run and make plays in space.

Ingredient 1: Recruiter

In my opinion, Pete Carroll is an amazing coach who embodies a lot of the parts of the ideal coach—so I'll go ahead and use him as an example for recruiting.

Pete has this incredible energy about him that's contagious. Plus the confidence he has in himself and his team is off the charts. Pete tells me he walks into a player's home and isn't there to tell him that he's going to redshirt as a freshman. I don't know of any coach out there who makes that pitch to an entire class. Sure, some will say to a surefire hit, like '08 sensational recruit Terrell Pryor, that he would play right away. But to tell all your recruits that you plan on playing them right away is unique. Pete's theory is that he wants guys who are ready to go—that pitch is a magnet for the super blue-chippers out there who want to play as freshmen. If you're really good, you're thinking that you should be a part of the Trojans team from day one.

And the fact that Pete can say he's been a head coach in the NFL is comforting to players, assuring them that he does indeed know what it takes to get them ready to play on Sundays.

Florida coach Urban Meyer has a slightly different persona but the same oomph in his pitch. His success in 2008 has put the Florida Gators in that class with USC: two championships in three years. Kids he's talking to think they are the best of the best. Meyer's pitch to kids is for them to look at his track record. His first head coaching stop was in 2001 at Bowling Green, where he immediately earned Coach of the Year honors. Meyer's next stop was in 2003 at Utah, where the team went 10–2 his first season there. In 2004 he followed it up with a perfect 12–0 record, including a win in the Fiesta Bowl over Pittsburgh.

I tell you about Meyer's short history and his amazing winning record because it is a powerful testimony to give when he's in front of a talented kid and his parents. Meyer's record, along with his offense that spreads the field for both running and passing, is something that all blue-chip recruits desire to be a part of. Unlike my first college coach, Ron Meyer, whom we called Golden Tongue, Urban looks at you with a confident glare that just screams out loud that he's a winner.

Both Carroll and Meyer are getting the cream of the crop, but both possess different approaches on the sidelines. Go to a game and you'll see Pete out on the field playing catch with his son, who, by the way, coaches at USC, too. Check out Urban before a game and you'll see these steely eyes peering over his squad making sure the boys are ready to go. At the end of the day, both schools have incredible talent, so their winning records are no surprise.

I also like the approach of Mack Brown at Texas and Jim Tressel at Ohio State. They too have loads of really talented players, but their pitch to prospects comes more from a mentor/dad role. Mack is Mr. Down Home, and he keeps it real with moms, dads, and players. He and Tressel remind me a lot of each other in their styles.

Nick Saban at Alabama has a big stick to swing when he walks into a recruit's house—he won a national championship at LSU and appears headed in the right direction at Alabama, too. Saban has that same look as Urban Meyer—that winning is it and nothing else matters. That attitude is contagious to the team. How many times have we seen Saban coaching or doing an interview and seen the intensity with which he delivers answers? If you play for Saban, you'd better never show up half-cocked because I guarantee you, he won't be half-cocked.

Sometimes while recruiting you need to be bold even though you might have just followed one of the above coaches into a house and are competing with the likes of Pete Carroll for a player. For that, I like Rick Neuheisel. Rick's not afraid of anything or anybody. I love that and have complete confidence that if I were his athletic director, I could sleep comfortably at night knowing that Rick isn't being intimidated by anyone or any school in the recruiting wars. I can hear Rick now pitching a player hard who's just seen USC, Florida, and Texas, and telling him he needs to go to UCLA to help the Bruins win the Pac-10 title and play for the national championship.

Ingredient 2: Disciplinarian

Okay, so assume you've got some really talented players on your team. That means each one of those kids thinks he's three and done—three years removed from high school and he's off to the NFL. That means you've got a locker room full of egos and expectations. Many of these players have been told they are the second coming since they were in high school. The laws and rules don't apply to them, right? How many times when Lou Holtz was coaching did he bench a star player just before a *huge* game for disciplinary reasons? Lots of times—and it seems like his team always won even without their star.

In the 2008 season, Miami coach Randy Shannon benched his starting QB a couple of times for rules violations. I guarantee you, his team in that locker room supported and appreciated his doing the right thing for the team.

Joe Paterno has a reputation that is rock solid on this as well; his team understands that there are rules that must be obeyed. Same with Les Miles at LSU. I sat with Les during my spring tour, and we talked at length about his star QB, Ryan Perrilloux, who was at the time suspended and not able to go through spring practice with the team. Les knew that the kid had a good heart, but maybe needed some good ol' tough love to help him get his life in order. Keep in mind that LSU was coming off winning a national championship the year before and had a pretty darn good chance of a shot at another title with Perrilloux at QB. But the lure of winning games didn't distract Les from doing what was right for both the player and the team. History will show that Perrilloux was readmitted to the team only to blow it again, and that was it. He was dismissed from the team.

Now the Tigers had to deal with the loss of their star player for the season, and it proved to be more of a challenge than even I suspected it would be. The Tigers struggled in the win column but won big time in the "right thing to do" column.

How about Nick Saban suspending his All-American left tackle, Andre Smith, before the 2009 Sugar Bowl? Regardless of the reason, Saban believed it was the right thing to do for his team and for the university. Alabama got embarrassed and upset by Utah—who knows if Smith's presence would have made a difference? What I do know is that his exclusion from the game was a distraction for his teammates to deal with. But from that suspension and going forward, everybody on the Alabama team now knows that whatever Smith did was wrong and that if Saban will suspend an All-American like Smith, he'll darn sure do it to them, too. Parental love—sometimes tough love is best for all involved.

Ingredient 3: Politician

Maybe it could fall under the category of schmoozer or glad-hander, but a great coach knows the importance of taking care of business. There are three important branches he must continually be taking care of. First and foremost, he needs to please the athletic director—the person more than likely responsible for his hiring. Second on the to-do list is to make sure the university's president is in your corner. And last, but certainly not least, you need the support of the alumni base.

In general terms, it's easy for a coach to be close to his AD. Common sense says the two are joined at the hip and must win and graduate players or else they won't be in their positions for too long. It's imperative that the two have each other's backs. A really good example of this is at Louisville University, where Steve Kragthorpe is under heavy criticism from the media and fans for not winning. The AD, Tom Jurich, hired Steve and has been telling the alums and fans that the job Steve's doing is good and that the situation isn't what it appears to be on the outside. In other words, the team needs a lot of rebuilding and Steve is the guy to get it done. Steve's a heck of a coach, but if he hadn't kept up his relationship with Tom, well, he'd be adding to the unemployment line.

The coach also has to stay lined up with the academicians and the president of the school. Look no further than Joe Paterno to see what that means to your longevity as a head football coach.

Now, I'm not saying Joe Pa's around because he's close to the administration, but I have no doubt that he's had total school support over the years while they weren't winning the Big Ten title.

Ingredient 4: X's and O's

Okay, so now I finally get down to the fact that I need my coach to have football knowledge. Crazy, isn't it? Gone are the days when you could just land Vince Lombardi, Tom Landry, or Don Shula and call it a day. Those coaches would go to the office early in the morning—assuming they went home in the first place—and stay there all day watching film, meeting with coaches and players, and then going to practice. They'd eat and study some more—to heck with all the distractions that might have been around. Let me tell ya what: there are a lot of coaches out there who know football—a heck of a lot more who fit this category than the ingredients previously talked about.

Let's start with a guy who loves pirates—Texas Tech's Mike Leach. Mike says he loves the history of pirates and how they were actually very disciplined. Each had their own role, and it was important to work as a team in order to be successful. Mike's a perfect example of a coach who knows offense, but doesn't wake up each morning thinking about shaking hands down at the local diner or QB club or Rotary Club meeting. It will be interesting to see if Leach can keep his offense rolling now that his teams are on the national radar.

Speaking of Texas Tech, the team I just watched them lose to in the 2009 Cotton Bowl was the Rebels of Ole Miss. Their coach, Houston Nutt, is outstanding. I've always admired how Houston found ways to get the ball in the hands of his playmakers. Remember when Nutt was at Arkansas and they had Darren McFadden? Nutt put McFadden in the shotgun to take a direct

snap from center—he called it the Wildcat formation. It dominated defenses. Now we see teams all over the country putting
their star runners in the shotgun. Heck, I've even seen it being
run in the NFL.

It's hard to ignore the success Pete Carroll has had with his
defenses out west at USC. It seems that year in and year out, they
not only have great players, but they also come up with game
plans to dominate their opponents. I watched it this year in the
2009 Rose Bowl against a very explosive and high-scoring Nittany
Lions team. The Trojans allowed some meaningless points late in
the second half en route to another brilliant statistical season.

I'll give you a name that's not generally out there yet on the
national radar: Baylor Bears coach Art Briles. I've watched Art
coach in games and attended his practices, too. The man knows
football and how to teach it. Art's a competitive guy who will
knock off a bunch of teams with more talent than he has because
he gets everything out of his ball club. Many coaches talk about
doing the little things right. Briles makes 'em do it right! Plus,
he connects personally with his players—a very important trait if
you want to get the most out of your athletes.

A few years ago I was watching Briles while he was head coach
of the Houston Cougars. A new NCAA rule had been put in place
moving the spot of the kickoff back 5 yards. It was designed to
allow more returns and fewer kicks going into the end zone, which
was going to put a lot of pressure on kick-coverage teams to make
plays in open space. I watched Briles and his staff coach a drill
where his cover team was learning how to go down the field staying
in their assigned lane, take on a blocker and get rid of 'em, then get
back in their coverage lane. Think of kickoff coverage lanes as the
kick coverage team going down the field creating a fishnet that's
got to cover from sideline to sideline. If a player loses his lane, the
return man has a huge hole in the net to go through.

Briles was practicing the little things, and his team was better for it. Baylor better hope a big job doesn't open up anytime soon that's interesting to Art. He's a good one for sure.

Ingredient 5: Played at the School

I know this is somewhat of a reach, but I love the coaches who are coaching at their alma maters. These coaches have spilled their own blood on the field for their schools and will have a sense of pride to get the job done. A classic example of that was Rich Rodriguez when he was at West Virginia. Rich led the Mountaineers to become one of the best programs in all of college football. Now I realize his departure from there to Michigan was hotly contested, but Rich did a heck of a job of propping up his old school before he left.

Mike Gundy's well on his way to doing the same thing at his old school, Oklahoma State. Mike was a QB in the '80s and is a young go-getter who recruits very well.

That's another bonus for having a coach with blood ties to the school—they can say with certainty to a mom, a dad, and a player that they went to the school and had a great experience. They aren't asking the kid to do something they didn't do.

Rick Neuheisel out at UCLA is another example: I've already praised him earlier and he's a great fit for the Bruins, having been a former QB for their squad.

And how's this for a great example? Frank Beamer at Virginia Tech. Beamer is one of my favorite coaches out there. He's got loads of qualities we've been going over, and his love for the school is second to none. The Hokies are year in and year out a good football team. Entering the 2008 season, the Hokies had a lot of questions to answer. Boy, did they ever answer them.

The team made it through a transition phase of the season to earn a spot in the ACC championship game. They won the ACC and then went on to a victory in the Orange Bowl against Cincinnati, finishing the year 10–4. I'm telling you: Beamer's passion and love for his school is real and it's a benefit for the Hokies.

•   •   •

So who is the ideal coach? No straddling the fence here by me: I've deliberated this for a long time because there are so many qualified to choose from. But I'm going with Pete Carroll. For the reasons I've stated earlier, he is excellent in each category except the alma mater one (Pete went to the University of the Pacific.)

Seeing Carroll and his Trojans this spring and seeing the fire in his step was contagious to everyone around him. Being in the huddle with Pete explaining what he was about to run, hearing the fire in his voice, the confidence in what he was doing was obvious.

Pete wasn't a high-powered player in college. After high school he attended the College of Marin, a junior college where he played safety. After junior college, he went on to be an all-league performer for the University of the Pacific. I like reading about his past because it gives me a feel for why he's so successful. Obviously, Pete was determined to make it in sports. He's got what us boys down in the South call moxie, meaning he's big on desire but short on overall talent.

I laugh because, as competitive as he is, he'd probably debate me on his skill set. For the record, Pete, I did see where you were all-conference and had a cup of coffee with the old World

Football League and its Honolulu Hawaiians. Still, it sounds like you were a player with a lot of moxie!

Doesn't it speak volumes about Carroll as a coach and his program that in LA he's able to go red carpet wherever he chooses? If he keeps up the pace he's going with in winning Pac-10 titles, USC will make him an honorary graduate before long. And that's why I think Pete Carroll is the perfect coach.

THE WACKY WORLD OF COLLEGE FOOTBALL

I should have known after the opening weekend that this would be a wild year.

UCLA knocking off Tennessee, 27–24, was a total surprise to me.

I mentioned earlier in my diary during the spring tour that UCLA wasn't one of the more talented teams I had seen in the spring. I didn't visit Tennessee, but rest assured, they have more talent running around Rocky Top than the Bruins had on September 1, 2008—the night UCLA upset 'em.

As I look back on that game, there was this undercurrent of good vibes and bad vibes taking place that we couldn't really see, but I could certainly feel. Rick Neuheisel and his team were full of hope and excitement. On the other sideline, you had Phillip Fulmer and his Vols "talking" about how they were going to do this and that. How many times have you heard the saying "Talk is cheap?" It's true. What we should continue to be mindful of is how important team chemistry is in terms of how well a team is going to do *on* the field. I'm not saying Fulmer isn't a good coach or doesn't focus on these aspects. The man certainly wins a lot of games. But all I know is that on that night, UCLA looked like a team, whereas Tennessee looked like a collection of players.

Remember my visit to Texas, the other UT, in the spring? They were as talented as the Vols, but they were working on team unity and cohesiveness as much as they were on execution of plays. No doubt all coaches will tell you that they, too, are into chemistry and teamwork. But these elusive assets aren't something you can buy at the local sporting goods store. More times than not, they're the result of a coach recruiting good character and having players on the team who are solid leaders. Plus, I believe it's imperative that your superstar is a hard worker who leads by example.

For me personally, this was going to be perhaps the most challenging year of my broadcasting career. My daughters, Jessica and Caylin, had already graduated from college, so I wasn't missing any events that were going on with them. But my boys were in the thick of football. Adam was going to be a redshirt freshman receiver at Texas Tech, and Andy was entering his senior season of high school as a receiver.

Andy played his games on Friday nights, so for me to see him play meant that I had to go home early Friday morning after doing my game on Thursday night and then catch the first flight out on Saturday in order to get back to New York for my ABC studio work. That was a pretty big risk because if there was bad weather or an issue with the plane, I'd more than likely miss my Saturday studio shows. If that had happened, I wouldn't have had to worry about missing games—I'd have been fired and been a full-time dad/fan.

For Adam, getting to see him in person was more than likely not going to happen. With my Thursday night games and my ABC studio work in New York each Saturday, unless my bosses allowed me to miss a day in New York to personally call a Texas Tech game, I had no shot of seeing him play in person. My only hope was that Tech would pull off a great season and therefore have most, if not all, of their games on TV. And if that happened, I'd be doing the pregame and halftime shows from New York for their games.

AUGUST 15, 2008

I've started doing the annual preseason sports talk radio tour around the country. It's a pretty cool tradition for me.

Kind of kick starts the season with the fans. I can hear the intensity and local passion each station and their hosts have for the upcoming season. If I'm on in Atlanta, they're dialed in big-time with the SEC for sure. These hosts/callers are even more aware of Georgia and Georgia Tech. The radio stations in Atlanta have drunk the Kool-Aid and think UGA will win it all. Most are skeptical, though, of the results they expect from first-year coach Paul Johnson at Georgia Tech.

Out West, the callers and fans are all about USC. Why not? That's a pretty decent bet for being right. I'm already hearing from Pac-10 fans that "we," the media, never give their conference any love or respect. I laugh to myself and wonder if they'd taken the time to follow my weekly vote on the AP Poll. If they did, they'd know I love USC and have 'em #1.

It's been interesting to hear how most everybody is cool and understanding that Rich Rodriguez and his new team, the Michigan Wolverines, will struggle in '08 until they can find a QB. I laugh inside at their "understanding," wondering if they know just how far off they are from being a Big Ten challenger. I think back to my spring visit with Big Blue and just remember leaving there telling people that it was like Coach Rod and his staff were speaking French even though the Wolverines players only understood Spanish! Yes siree, what they had there was a failure to communicate!

Radio callers from the Southwest are all over the board about who's going to win the Big 12. Their biases are clear—Austin callers love their Horns; Norman, OK, loves the Sooners; and out in Lubbock, the Red Raiders faithful believe this is their year. There's even a number of fans who like Missouri's chances with Chase Daniel at QB. Daniel, after all, was coming off a top-five Heisman run in '07, and the Tigers had ten starters returning on defense.

Now that I look back on this diary, I'm reminded that fans and media members are all really in the dark about what their teams are going to be prior to a new season. We are all victims of the same error in how we analyze a team's chances for an upcoming season. As the calendar clicks by, somewhere around the first of July we begin to think about college football. The first time we see a preseason print publication on the newsstands, we buy it. These magazines do nothing more than pick up on the themes we'd been talking about at the end of the previous season. It's hard for them to pick up on any new developments during the spring. Oh, they'll tell us how they've got beat writers all over the country and how their information is solid and dead-on. Hogwash! Ninety-nine percent of print writers couldn't draw up a formation if their lives depended on it. Yet these same writers are rating and judging teams and predicting how they are going to do?

I know I'm firing up a band of writers out there who will take this personally, but it's not meant as an insult. An insult would be those writers out there believing they understand football strategy and how to evaluate a team's strengths and weaknesses after never having played a down of football! Just as it would be an insult to think a coach could write a newspaper column.

I'll never forget the time when I was a New England Patriots player and our first-ballot Hall of Famer John Hannah aggressively challenged a local Boston beat writer regarding the "grade" this writer had given our team after a game. You know the report cards I'm talking about—local writers give a grade to each unit of the team on how they performed the day before. Hannah led this reporter to the drawing board and asked/demanded that he draw up a 4–3 defense and name the positions in it. And then do the same with a 3–4 alignment. The writer pooped his pants and couldn't do it. But this guy was worthy/credible enough to grade our performance?

During a call-in show in Atlanta, most all of the callers were certain that Georgia was going to play for the national title. They were basing their beliefs on how the 2007 season had ended. We (me included) assumed (ass-outta-u-and-me) that UGA, with their all-star QB and running back, along with having most of their defenders back, would be the team to beat. My late 2007 assumption was revised once I had seen UGA during the spring and realized that, compared to the other schools I'd already seen practice, their collection of players were good but not nearly good enough to handle their upcoming schedule.

The entire month of September used to be when teams were working toward finalizing their rosters and positions for players. Rotations and playing time were being put together, and coaches worked out the kinks in their pre-conference games. But that month-long luxury is out the window nowadays. A case in point was in 2007 when fifth-ranked Michigan lost at home to Appalachian State. It's a game that will live in college football lore—the upset was so amazing that Michigan dropped twenty-one spots and fell completely out of the AP Top 25. It was the largest drop ever by a ranked team.

Looking back on that upset, it was the initial shot-heard-round-college-football alerting the big boys that they weren't the only teams who had good players. Unfortunately for Michigan and their coach, Lloyd Carr, they faced a perfect storm in Appalachian State—a team with a good coaching staff, the spread offense, and players making plays they weren't suppose to make. And by the time Michigan realized that the game wasn't going to be a cakewalk, it was too late.

Coaches around the country used that example for the rest of 2007 to talk to their teams about being ready to play "inferior" teams on their upcoming schedules. Further bulletin-board material was provided by teams in 2007, as a remarkable *thirteen* unranked teams beat top-five opponents!

The 2008 season was not going to be any different, with plenty of early matchups that would continue parity's wide swath being cut across college football.

For instance, on August 30, 2008, Alabama played ninth-ranked Clemson. The Tigers were going to be great . . . on paper. Alabama, on the other hand, was full of young players and had some growing up to do. Boy, was I off on my expectations for the Tide. The game can be summed up like this: Alabama went from being breast-fed to drinking soda in sixty minutes of game time. They traded cribs with Clemson, which went from solid foods back to the bottle in those same sixty minutes.

Now, several of my Clemson friends would debate us which type of bottle they went to, but regardless of the liquid, the Tigers were exposed. Alabama and the SEC once again reared up and displayed their fast physical style of football and sent a reassuring message to the rest of the country that you just don't mess with the boys down South in the SEC. Know what I mean, Verne?

APRIL 8, 2008

My daughter Caylin graduated from Texas A&M, so I've spent a lot of time around the Aggies and love 'em. I went by to see the Aggie practice and couldn't believe what I saw . . . or didn't see. The Aggies have a talented coaching staff led by former Aggie assistant and Green Bay Packer head coach Mike Sherman. But in all of my years of playing against the Aggies and following them as an Aggie parent, I've never seen them with a talent level as low as it is. I'll put it to ya this way: the Aggies have as much room to grow as any team I visited in the country.

It was a warm day in College Station but not summer hot. I was standing by the linebackers watching them go through individual period, which is when players are by themselves with their position coach working on technique or specific assignments or even drills in general. This particular period lasted no more than ten minutes. At the end of that ten-minute session not only were the linebackers tired but so were their teammates. Since they had just come out of offseason conditioning, I'd expected to at least see a team that was in shape. Maybe they were . . . maybe I caught 'em on a bad day.

Side note: a little research later did tell me the school had their traditional Chili Cookoff over the previous weekend. For those who haven't been to a Chili Cookoff, I highly recommend attending one. It is what it sounds like. Cooks bring their best chili and food to the event to be judged. And with all that eating there needs to be plenty of fluids to wash down the tastin'. Most of the drinks consumed tend to dull the taste buds by the end of the day! That ol' saying that you can't soar with the eagles and hoot with the owls at the same time is absolutely true.

So there ya go—a little background on the Aggies, a team that was playing on August 30 as well. They were completely on the other end of the rankings spectrum from the top teams in the country, but nonetheless, it was a huge game for the Aggies. They were playing at home against Arkansas State. That would be *Sshtate* (as it's often pronounced by Jesse Palmer), a mighty representative out of the Sun Belt conference taking on A&M in College Station. Please know that I'm kidding when I say "mighty"; sure, it's a good conference, but it's not even close to the Big 12. It was Mike Sherman's first game and everybody had plenty of expectations for his team—at least for this particular game. This was supposed to be the game that would lead to many more wins during the '08 season. After all, it was a safe bet that there wasn't a player on Arkansas State that was even recruited by Texas A&M.

In addition, you would be amazed if you ever saw the Aggies' campus—amazed at all the money that has been spent on athletic facilities. You've heard me rave about the look and style and plush amenities of Texas, Ohio State, Michigan, and Notre Dame. Well, the Aggies are in that same league. The Aggies recently built a practice bubble for the team to use on bad-weather days. This bubble is monstrous in size and engulfs well more than a hundred yards. My guess is that bubble facility alone costs more than the entire annual football budget at Arkansas State. Do you get my point here? This isn't an apples-to-apples comparison of programs; this is an example of haves and have-nots.

You've probably gathered what I'm leading up to here. *Sshtate* beat the Aggies 18–14 and shocked the Aggie faithful. When I called my daughter Caylin to talk about the game, she said she couldn't believe they just lost to Arkansas State. Neither could the rest of the Aggies and their millions of fans. Even I was surprised despite knowing the Ags were going to struggle in '08. I'd been telling my Aggie buddies to get ready for a rough season, but I had no inkling that this was going to happen.

Using this game as an illustration of early season surprises in 2008 is important to understanding that particular season, but it also serves to underscore the year-in and year-out reality that college football has parity among the schools in ways we've never seen before.

A lot of that has to do with passion by players at schools like Arkansas State to prove themselves when playing against a "big" school that had passed on them out of high school. In this matchup, Arkansas State beat the Aggies by outhustling and executing better than the Aggies. And while the players of the winning team were a little shorter, weighed less, and were definitely not as fast, they played the game with more intensity and passion. I will say many times throughout this book that evaluating players in high school by college coaches is an inexact science at best. My friend and defensive coordinator at Penn State, Tom Bradley, openly admits that to me. So many times coaches forget to watch and see how a kid plays the game. Is he around the ball making plays? Does he always seem to break tackles? Things like that. I respect Tom for his candor, because most coaches think they actually know who's got it and who hasn't.

Speaking of who hasn't got it: on opening weekend '08, Michigan was hosting Utah, a team that has been good over the last few years, but one that couldn't even be mentioned in the same breath as all-time programs like Big Blue. I'd spoken with Coach Rodriguez about his team, and he had said they were working hard and that he was cautiously optimistic.

Coach Rodriguez had won three Big East titles and posted the first back-to-back top-10 finishes in school history for West Virginia, his alma mater. Rich is widely respected for his coaching of the wide-open offense highlighted by the QB-read option. Basically, he specializes in an offense that needs a QB who can run like the wind and yet pull up and pass when the defense loads up to stop the run. Rich had that at West Virginia with all-everything QB Pat White.

That's one reason Michigan was so eager to hand over millions of dollars to Rich to get him to leave his alma mater and come to Michigan to change the offense and to make it "hip" and up-to-date like Florida, Texas, Oregon, and other top programs out there. This hiring and new offensive philosophy would be totally different for Michigan and the Big Ten. The old days of 3 yards and a cloud of dust were about to be gone. But as my old friend Corso says, "Not so fast, my friend!"

Remember my ingredients for a perfect coach and how recruiting was at the top of the list? In order for Rich and Michigan to be good, they need a QB like Pat White. Pure and simple as that—and in 2008, Michigan didn't have a cupboard of QBs to choose from, since their QBs had been recruited to hand the ball off or drop back in the pocket as passers. There weren't any speedy runners hanging around Ann Arbor, Michigan, waiting for Rich's offense to show up.

You can imagine what I'm leading up to here. Utah did in fact go on to beat Michigan. As the world found out, at least Michigan had lost to a good team. This wasn't like the Aggies losing to Arkansas State. Utah was the original Bowl Championship Series (BCS) party crasher. Let me explain.

The simplest explanation of the BCS is that it was initially set up for the top schools to play in the major bowls: Sugar, Fiesta, Rose, and Orange—these schools would come from the major conferences plus perhaps Notre Dame. The major conferences were the Big East, ACC, SEC, Big 12, Big Ten, and Pac-10. Notre Dame was allowed to be part of the process since they once were—notice I say "were"—a big-time winning program. I'll go much deeper into this BCS topic in chapter 7, but I want to qualify that Utah was a good team.

Here's why: the Utes of Utah played in the 2005 Fiesta Bowl, beating Big East conference champion Pittsburgh. With the win at the Big House to start the season, Utah started their undefeated run, culminating in a Sugar Bowl win against number-3-ranked (on my ballot) Alabama. So it wasn't a fluke that Utah had beaten Michigan, but at the time no one was paying attention to the Utes and the Mountain West Conference.

But the real relevance of my highlighting the Michigan loss here is to focus on the beginning of a new chapter in Big Blue's storied history. Sure, they've been mediocre for the last couple of years, but once Coach Rodriguez is able to get his types of players in there, Michigan has every right to believe they will improve and be back on top.

As for me on the home front, opening weekend went great. Adam got his first collegiate catch at home against Eastern Washington, and Andy opened up the season with a couple of great catches, too. Both games were transferred to me via text, with my wife, Marilyn, providing the play-by-play via her cell phone. I go wacky nuts waiting on updates from the boys' games—especially Andy's high school games, because I can't get scores or updates from anywhere else. I'm lucky Marilyn is a good sport and takes the time to keep me posted.

Week two was a little tricky for me with Adam. Texas Tech was playing at Nevada, and the game wasn't being shown on TV. It was a late kickoff—8:00 West Coast time. That made it 11:00 Eastern time, and I was in New York just finishing up my ABC studio work. So here's the visual: I ran out of the studio and across the street to my hotel, hoofed it upstairs to my room, and turned on my computer to listen to the game on the Internet. It took me almost half a quarter to get the darned thing working; I had to buy this season package and all kinds of junk. I pulled a chair up next to my computer and held my head down next to it so I could hear the announcers. I had the usual street noise of New York City below: horns, fire trucks, police cars, jackhammers, and people all sounding as if they were in the room with me. My adrenaline was flying as I sat there waiting to hear Adam's name called out.

Tech scored on a pass, and the announcer said, "Great catch and run by Michael Crabtree and an excellent block downfield by Adam James." I let out a huge "Yeah! Atta boy!" The people in the room next door probably thought I'd either gone nuts or was one happy honeymooner!

I finished listening to the game around 2:30 in the morning, then jumped into bed for a quick sleep because my car service was picking me up at 5:30 to go to the airport. I'll never forget listening to that game on my computer in my room. It was one of those crazy parental moments.

• • •

Earlier I showed you my preseason top-25 poll with a comment next to each team as to what I was thinking when I put the ballot

---

September 29 Ballot

1. USC
2. Florida
3. OU
4. LSU
5. Georgia (Ohio St. fell out of top 5 & was replaced by Georgia)
6. Missouri
7. Wisconsin
8. Alabama: Not even on radar in preseason top 25—oops!
9. Ohio State
10. Texas Tech
11. Texas

---

12. Penn State: Up from #22—well-coached & team chemistry
13. Auburn: Lost to LSU close but concerned w/lack of offense
14. Wake Forest: Another great job by Jim Grobe
15. South Florida
16. BYU
17. Kansas
18. Vanderbilt: Hello, Vandy!
19. Utah: Not in preseason rankings
20. Oklahoma State: Powerful offense
21. Colorado: Nice start w/win over West Virginia
22. Clemson: Fading fast
23. Fresno State
24. Michigan State
25. Boise State: Very solid team

together. Here ya go with ballot number two after the first round of games.

No doubt one of the more interesting teams to follow in 2008 was the Irish of Notre Dame. As I've already stated, my spring visit had me believing that the Irish were going to be the Cinderella story of 2008. As they worked their way through the September matchups, I was reminded of my sit-down visit with Charlie Weis back in the spring when we walked through the schedule. "We should beat San Diego State; we're catching Michigan with a new offense and head coach so we should win here; we're at Michigan State but being 2–0 and playing well I'm gonna say we win there; then we come back home for Purdue and we're supposed to win that one, too."

I agreed with his evaluation at the time.

Things started out as planned as the Irish opened up with two wins before heading to their toughest game of September. But it wasn't to be, as the Irish's offense just couldn't get on track and they lost to Michigan State. Beating Purdue at home the following week was a must because leaving September on a two-game losing streak would have opened the door for lots of criticism from not only the media but also the Irish faithful. ND and their coach took care of Purdue to finish September with a respectable 3–1 record. I was still on board for a possible Irish storybook run, but the unplanned loss to Michigan State had me wondering a little bit as to whether or not I was wrong in my assessment of the team's chances to wear the glass slipper at the end of the season.

The little things I was following that would indicate signs of improvement were apparent in areas like the offensive line. The Irish line in the past (when the name Notre Dame still meant something) was awesome! Big men up front, like All-American Aaron Taylor, led the way to many Irish victories. The 2007 Irish offensive line set a record, but one that they'd rather not have had the honor of owning: the unit allowed 58 QB sacks. Ugly, to say the least. No way the team will be able to accomplish anything until they improve on protecting the QB. Well, through the first two games of 2008, they hadn't given up a single sack.

•   •   •

I've mentioned how early-season games can impact the entire season. Each year we see it happen, and the '08 season was no different. Two games in late September that would be monumental in determining who would play for the national championship showed up on the schedule: a Thursday night game with USC at

Oregon State and, two days later, Ole Miss playing at the Swamp against the Florida Gators.

One of the many things I like about college football is that you never know when a special week will happen. I mean, it's easy to look at the weekend lineup of games and determine on paper what will be good matchups and which weekends won't be as exciting. This last week of September games didn't make you want to throw a *GameDay* watching party.

Each year around late winter/early spring, I get our Thursday night schedule. As soon as I saw that USC was playing at Oregon State on September 25, 2008, I was excited. Any time you get USC on TV it's a bonus. I'd never been to a game in Corvallis, Oregon, so I was fired up about seeing a game there, too. The only bummer about the matchup in my mind was the potential for it being a blowout. Would the Beavers of Oregon State be able to hang in there and give us a respectable game?

That's always a concern for announcers. The last thing we want is a rout. Two things happen during bad games: first, you lose your audience; second, after a while nobody cares about what's going on down on the field, so you'd better be way over-prepared with material so you have something to say,

One of the first things I learned about doing a game in Corvallis was that it isn't easy to get to. Our crew usually arrives at the game site early Wednesday morning. But we all decided to hook up in Portland, Oregon, on Tuesday night, so we could make the hour-and-a-half drive early enough on Wednesday to do our prep at Oregon State. I'll talk more later about our Thursday routine and explain why leaving on Tuesday is a killer for our overall prep for the entire week. (One thing it does is add another night on the road, which makes for a really long week.)

So on Tuesday afternoon, before I flew out, we had our conference call with the USC coaching staff and players. It's a routine: we have Monday or Tuesday conference calls with the traveling teams, and we meet with the home team on Wednesday at their site. I'll share with you my notes from the USC meetings so you'll get a feel for what I was hearing going in. Plus, I'll add my comments regarding the film study of both teams. These notes are what I believed were the main bullet points of our conversations heading into the game—things I needed to use and follow during the game to see if they were happening.

USC: PETE CARROLL, HEAD COACH

- says he's the last one who'll make comparisons to previous teams or units, but the key to being good on defense is to create turnovers. Off to a good start—it's a personality-driven defense with linebackers Brian Cushing, Ray Mauluga; the players feed off each other. *Excitement* is key.
- says another key to great defense is awareness . . . another level by this unit. They understand philosophy and strategy.
- stressed again level of play of linebackers being very high, a real impact on team.
- he said his offensive line is good because they have to go against their defensive teammates in practice.
- big point on how this is the first time he's had his entire staff back together . . . continuity and that all of his assistants are really good coaches.
- says he never mentions "Big Game" . . . doesn't believe in hyping a game as one bigger than the other . . . he laughs at hype.
- **says his team didn't play great last game vs Ohio State!
- made a point that he never wants one of his players to think they have to play above their head or think they

have to be something they aren't. Pete tells his players to just be themselves because that is all they need to be . . . don't go above and beyond.

- he's using a theme for this game . . . it's opening play in the Pac-10.

For me, coming out of that meeting with Pete, I was interested in a few things he said. Like how this particular defense seems to have a different level of awareness. In football terms, they understand not only their own responsibilities but also how that role plays into the larger picture with the other ten players on defense. It sounded to me like he was playing with eleven outstanding athletes who could be assistant coaches, too. That's freakin' scary when you think about it. Pete's had some very good defenses; as a matter of fact, when you think about it, when hasn't he had a good defense?

In regard to his assistant coaches, hearing him praise their level of work was impressive. It's always a sign of a good leader when he isn't afraid to acknowledge openly to the public how good the coaching staff is. Plus, isn't it even more impressive how Pete's been able to continue to win while at the same time dealing with coaching changes? We all know that winning breeds opportunity for assistants to move on; it's part of the gig.

How about when Pete said he never mentions "Big Game"? Very smart, because every week is the biggest game for USC's opponent and the Trojans have to be up for every game they play. Pete's smart to know that calling 'em all "Big" would be like the boy who cried wolf.

I put a double asterisk next to the comment about the Trojans not playing great against fifth-ranked Ohio State because they beat OSU 35–3! If that wasn't great, then what do we have to look forward to?

He then got into how he asks his team not to try anything above and beyond what they have. What a great thing to say to a locker room full of incredible talent. By saying that, he is reminding the players that they are the best and that it's the other team that has to play above and beyond their skills to beat USC.

USC: STEVE SARKISIAN, OFFENSIVE COORDINATOR

- lot of room to improve on offense . . . team's still young and learning, so they aren't on same page all the time when they're about to score.
- been telling the offense to prepare for a hostile environment.
- says new starting QB Mark Sanchez is the hardest working QB he's ever coached. Says Sanchez is first in to study film and hangs around until 11:00 P.M. Said he's a winner and championship guy. His leadership has been a pleasant surprise.
- making a point of emphasis this week to create more big plays.
- he's not surprised with his offensive line's success.
- regarding Oregon State . . . good defense, well-coached; puts their corners on an island one-on-one with receivers. Oregon State then uses safeties and linebackers to handle the middle of the field in pass coverage. So USC wants to see if they can't win the one-on-one opportunities.

My takeaway from my meeting with Sarkisian was that he knew Sanchez had the talent to lead his offense to a title. Here's a coach who's seen a couple of Trojans QBs win the Heisman: Carson

Palmer in 2002, whom he personally coached, and Matt Leinart in 2004, whom he followed closely during that season while he was the QB coach of the Oakland Raiders. So Sark knows what it takes for a QB to not only win but to be outstanding.

I was in LA the afternoon that Carroll made the announcement that the Trojans were naming Sanchez the starter for the 2008 season. I remember hanging around after practice and observing Sanchez and how he handled all the post-practice media and fan requests. I waited until he'd finished his business and then congratulated him on winning the starting job. Mark was very polite and confident that he'd be a winner for USC. Not just good but, as he told me on that spring day, he wanted to take his team to the Rose Bowl and for them to have a shot at playing for the national championship. Those are two lofty goals. Playing the Rose Bowl is something the team can control: they simply have to win their games during conference play. And this Oregon State matchup was the first on that slate. Playing for the national championship is far more complicated and not always in the hands of a team. All a team can do is win every game and hope for the best.

USC: NICK HOLT, DEFENSIVE COORDINATOR

- have to be aware that Oregon State likes to get the ball down the field.
- last year USC needed only four or five pass rushers to get pressure on Oregon State QB . . . a big plus that allowed more coverage.
- likes his defense and the depth they have. Says they are fresh because they can rotate so many bodies in the game.

- really expressed how good of an inside zone run team Oregon State is. Said his defensive tackles would have to hold up well against the run.
- impressed with young, talented runner Jacquizz Rodgers and his brother, slot receiver James Rodgers.
- believes QB Lyle Moevao is a dual threat . . . can run and pass.

Again, coming out of this meeting it was clear that Holt wasn't overlooking Oregon State. Nick was well aware of the talent and potential of the Beavers' running game. Of course, I hear it all the time from a coach: "We've got to stop the run first and foremost." Every coach I've ever met states that before every game as a key to winning. The overall tone of Holt's talk was like Carroll's—he was confident in his players and ready to go.

It was interesting to hear Holt single out true freshman running back Jacquizz Rodgers. I mean, come on! To me, Rodgers looked good on film, but he was just a freshman and he would be going against the Trojans' defense. Also take notice of the reference Holt made to the inside zone run as the top play for Oregon State. (As the game unfolded, this would be a major play used by the Beavers.)

I've always enjoyed that we get to meet with the two teams and hear from them how they plan to attack their opponent. There probably hasn't ever been a coach who designed a game plan they didn't think would work and give them a victory. And that's good. Obviously a coaching staff has to believe in their game plan or the team will have no shot at winning. Therefore, it's real important for announcers to keep that in mind as we prepare for the game.

I thoroughly enjoy listening to both teams' plans, taking my film study and observations into account, then seeing which staff/team was on track and whether I had accurately predicted what was going to happen.

As crazy as the 2008 season would be, my Thursday partners and I were off in our evaluations and picked the wrong team to win six of the first seven weeks! But that's why they play the games, right?

• • •

On Wednesday it was time for our meetings with Oregon State's players and coaches.

OREGON STATE: MIKE RILEY, HEAD COACH

- really excited about playing Thursday night on national TV against USC.
- recognizes USC will be jacked up, too, for Thursday night and doesn't expect them to overlook the Beavers.
- proud of his team for not giving up on season following earlier loss to Penn State . . . said his players have responded well to defeat and took experience of losing on the road to a really good team in front of loud home crowd.
- said USC is maybe the fastest they've ever been.
- defense of USC gets off blocks and back to the ball to make tackle . . . great pursuit defense that swarms and pressures opponents.
- has a lot of confidence in his players' ability to step up and compete even against USC.
- said his QB Lyle Moevao plays fast and makes good, quick decisions . . . said he'll have to in order to not get sacked or hit by USC.

- big discussion about how he was able to sign Jacquizz Rodgers out of Texas. Said when the coaches went to Houston area to recruit Quizz's high school, the coaches thought they were there to look at Quizz. The Oregon State coaches said no, they were there to see James Rodgers! The high school coaches said, Oh, well, he's good, too, but his younger brother Quizz is the real deal. Mike laughs at how the staff lucked out on not only James, who's a good player, but also how they got a starter the next year in his younger brother Quizz.

All right, here's my takeaway from Mike's meeting. In general, there's no doubt he was excited about playing and had this type of inner confidence in his team. Yeah, I could tell he was on edge a little bit—not short with us or anything, but maybe just anxious and ready to get on the field to see how the game would turn out. For me, visiting with Mike wasn't as productive regarding the X's and O's of the game, but what I was able to get from his body language and feelings he had for his team were extremely revealing.

OREGON STATE: DANNY LANGSDORF, OFFENSIVE COORDINATOR

- they're gonna have to move the QB pocket and get rid of the ball on time or they'll be sacked.
- must have balance . . . run the ball and throw it, too.
- preaches one-cut runs to his backs.
- USC likes to drop coverage and keep receivers in front of them.

- best Oregon State stuff: fly sweep and play-action. Key to fly sweep is timing of receiver in motion.
- he likes to have his motion receiver block and crack on linebackers.
- USC likes to change where they pressure from . . . last year hurt Beavers in middle of line.
- his offensive line is playing much better.
- must get ball off quickly when passing.

Danny was summing things up for us: USC is fast and gets to the ball. If Oregon State can't pick up different blitzes up front, then it will be a long night for his offense. The balance Danny talked about was going to be key. Take notice where he said that he preaches one-cut runs to his backs. For me, this was not only brilliant but an absolute must against any defense that is fast and gets off their blocks. Basically, he's saying that when a back starts to the line of scrimmage and makes his initial cut, he should stay with it. Unless you're Barry Sanders or Ladanian Tomlinson, that's pretty good advice.

Defenses like USC's are so fast that if your runner is dancing around in the backfield trying to cut here or there, the defense will surround the ball in no time. I see it all the time: a running back is lined up 7 yards back in the I formation, and by the time he gets to the line of scrimmage it looks like there's nowhere to go. But many times when you really study the film, you'll see that the offensive line initially had an opening for the runner, but the defense was so quick that what was there for a brief moment was gone in an instant. If that back had been a little closer to the line, say, maybe 6 yards deep, he might have hit the hole and there would have been a different result.

OREGON STATE: MARK BANKER, DEFENSIVE COORDINATOR

- impressed with USC QB Mark Sanchez being able to see the whole field and making good decisions.
- hurt last season by USC running backs running catching out and ups or wheel route, USC offensive line is so athletic and their scheme of turn-back protection forces defensive line to run around "wad" of lineman.
- secondary of Oregon State is experienced and good.
- believes in pressuring run game and pushing or spilling runners to another gap and teammate for tackle.
- Mark's been around Pac-10 and USC and is highly impressed with Pete Carroll's approach: recruit athletes and let 'em play . . . turn 'em loose. NFL-type approach to handling players.
- his defense works hard in practice to get to the ball.
- must match up well in zone coverage.
- slot receiver in crunch becomes the go-to guy for USC.

There was no doubt in my mind that Banker was prepared and ready for this game. The ultimate takeaway for me was how Mark said he's been around USC as a conference foe and so have his players, and they aren't in awe of or intimidated by the USC helmet or tradition. Mark's comments about that familiarity hit home for me in a big way. I see it in "big" games when a traditional powerhouse goes up against a team that's having a great year and trying to step up.

It happened to me at SMU my freshman year; we thought we were pretty good, then went up against highly ranked Texas . . . and they smoked us! The next season we were again thinking big and were playing at then second-ranked Texas. The helmet of the Horns got in our heads the year before. As a matter of fact, SMU had lost something like eighteen straight to Texas, so before the game started, our senior center stood up in the locker room and gave a speech. He talked about how we were talented and good and that the only thing standing between us and beating Texas was the logo on their helmet. He then lifted a small plastic replica UT helmet, *crushed* it between his hands, and said that helmet crap stops today!

My teammates and I flew out of the locker room and went on to beat Texas. It was the beginning of great things to come for us, but we had to get over that helmet thing.

As I listened to Mark Banker's thoughts on USC and how matter-of-fact he was in talking about them, I was reminded of my experience at SMU and that UT game. Oregon State players and Banker had great respect for USC, but they weren't in awe of them. Instead, the Beavers could reflect on how they'd beaten USC the last time the Trojans played in Corvallis in 2006.

That was 2006, however, and this was a different USC team.

My film study supported what both staffs were saying. This wasn't going to be a game of gadgets or tricks or new faces coming off the bench. The thing to watch for early on was whether or not Oregon State could handle the speed and athleticism of USC. Our production team and announcers were hoping that Oregon State would at least hang in there for a half. No doubt we all thought that USC would win.

Chris, Jesse, Erin, and I wanted to show the viewer examples of USC's power and speed and domination, why they'd be awfully hard to beat in 2008—or so we thought.

History shows that the results were completely different than what the notes and meetings and film study suggested. Oregon State looked like the team that would be hard to beat in 2008!

From the very beginning of the game, Oregon State looked the part. That means they weren't being blown away by anything—speed, athleticism, size, helmet logos—none of that business. The Beavers went about executing football plays and did a much better job of it than the Trojans.

Think back on my study notes from the coaches' meetings. USC defensive coordinator Nick Holt was dead on in respecting the offensive line of Oregon State and the running ability of Quizz Rodgers. Holt and the defense knew what play to expect from the Beavers. It wasn't tricky. Oregon State was bringing little 170-pound slot receiver James Rodgers in motion and at the snap of the ball he'd block out on the USC outside linebackers to keep them from crashing down inside to tackle his younger brother, Quizz. The offensive line was coming off man-to-man and blocking the Trojans' defensive line. Simple stuff, really; nothing unique about the strategy.

What was unique was the poor tackling by USC's defense.

Quizz Rodgers might be all of 5 feet 6 inches, and the Trojans defense wasn't dropping their butts low enough to tackle him. Two or three times the Trojans defense was called for a face mask penalty or was seen trying to tackle Quizz around the shoulder pads. It was a classic example of a running back being so low to the ground that the defender isn't used to having such a low strike point, and that's where the dropping of the fanny comes into play. The natural instinct and reaction of the tacklers weren't up to (or should I say down to?) the proper tackling area of a running back.

What's the proper tackling area? At the end of the play, the goal is to get the runner to the ground. And that's usually done a lot easier if a runner's legs are wrapped up or if the runner is hit so hard in the upper body that his legs can't keep him up. Generally, tackling the helmet of a runner isn't successful, just as it wasn't that night for the Trojans' defenders.

This late-September upset of USC turned out to be maybe the game of the year. At game time, the Trojans were the number-1 team in the country. After the game, they dropped to number 8 on my ballot. From this point on, the Trojans would have to hope for a lot of things to happen in order for them to get back in the one or two slot for a shot at the national championship. At this point in the season, of course, the goal was to simply pick up the pieces from this devastating loss and hope to win the Pac-10 title.

That's why I said earlier that the one thing the Trojans could control was to try to win the Pac-10 title and take a trip to the Rose Bowl. The national championship would be left to the computer algorithms of the BCS rankings. This was a theme Pete Carroll would adopt for his team the rest of the season.

Here's where I open myself up for considerable jabbing. I didn't have Oregon State ranked going into that game. They'd gotten beaten by lowly Stanford, been ripped apart at Penn State, and had beaten a Hawaii team, which meant nothing to me. With it being so early in the season, and them at 2–2, I couldn't get over the two losses. Yes, they'd just beaten number-1 USC, but at this point in the season there were a lot of teams still unbeaten or with only one loss who, because of their body of early work, deserved to be ranked ahead of Oregon State. As I write this and reflect back on the impressive win by the Beavers, I almost wonder to myself why I didn't rank them after watching the win. But if I go back and reflect on Oregon State as a whole on the season and stick to my evaluation process, they didn't deserve *yet* to be ranked in the top 25, even though they upset USC.

The other unlikely pivotal game of the year happened two days later down in Gainesville, Florida. The Gators were playing Ole Miss, and even though the Rebels were a decent team, nobody could have predicted with any level of credibility that the Gators would lose.

I've covered many games at the Swamp and have a standing agreement with myself that I'll not pick against Florida when they are at home. I've been burned in the past by picking against them there. The place is electric and crazy loud. It just seems to engulf an opposing team. Even if the Gators aren't playing well, their fans have the energy to pull them out of a loss.

The first encounter I had with the Swamp was back in 1991, when Steve Spurrier's boys beat up the Tennessee Vols pretty good. It was a great atmosphere, so loud I couldn't hear myself give a report from the field during the game.

So here we were in 2008, and no way I thought the Gators would lose to Ole Miss. The reasons for the loss aren't important. (Ole Miss made more plays and won the game by one point.) The loss to the Rebels that day, however, created a rather interesting pledge by the Gators to follow the rest of the season.

After the game, the standing Heisman Trophy winner from 2007, QB Tim Tebow, entered the press conference to answer questions about his team's loss. At some point during the press conference, Tebow made a statement that for the Gator nation was like listening to Moses convince his followers that he could part the Red Sea. For non-Gators fans, it was pretty comical and amusing. Tebow went on a rant, apologizing to the Gators fans about how he was sorry for his performance and how he'd never let something like that happen again. He assured the Gator nation that he would do everything in his power to make sure he and his teammates worked harder than anybody else. Tebow got so into it that he broke down in tears as he made his feelings known to the media and fans.

Obviously, when the Heisman trophy QB goes off like that, it's going to get a lot of exposure by the media. I have to say it got my attention. At the time, I felt sorry for the young man. I didn't care about the loss. It meant nothing to me. It was a big-time loss, but it was just a football game. The Gators were the second-ranked team in the country and they'd lost. But I felt for Tebow and called him the next day to try and cheer him up. Tim was still bummed, and I told him that he shouldn't feel that great of a load and responsibility for the team's loss.

He agreed, but it didn't make him feel any better. Tim said he was on the way over to the football facilities for a team meeting and was going to speak to his teammates about his goal and desire to outwork the rest of their opponents. I told him I admired him for his commitment to excellence, his team leadership, and for his personal standing for the Lord Jesus Christ. I wasn't calling as a media member, just as a fan/friend. Tim had been kind enough during my spring tour to have dinner with me, and I appreciated that.

So the stage was set to see if Tebow's pledge would be fulfilled. Would the Gators be able to recover and earn a trip to the SEC championship game? Were their national championship hopes dashed, just like USC's?

Isn't college football great? In the same week we had number 1 and number 2 go down in defeat. Let the comebacks begin!

7

IF IT'S BROKE...
FIX IT!

Political pressure from Washington, D.C., combined with an economic tsunami, has created the perfect storm for change in college football. If the sport is to change in our lifetime, on its own terms, then now is the time. If you don't remember anything else from this book, I hope you'll at least remember that the economics of college football are in bad shape, too. We might not be seeing it yet, but the undercurrent is flowing strong, and it's not a good flow for the majority of athletic departments.

As we say here in Texas, "It's time to talk a little *bid-ness*."

I've been saying for years that I'm in favor of a playoff system to determine who wins the national championship. As of the writing of this book, and in the midst of the worst recession/economy in my lifetime, the tides of change for a playoff are becoming more realistic with each negative economic report.

It's been said for years that there was no way any of us in our lifetimes would see a playoff system for college football. Not so fast, my friend (thanks, Lee)! Drastic times, combined with political pressure, just might do the trick.

Let me take you back to when I was in the sixth grade. This is really against my nature, but for a moment I'm going to brag a little bit. I was living in Pasadena, Texas; the locals call it "Stink-a-dena" because of the smell that's in the air. Pasadena is around the part of Houston where you have lots of oil/gas refineries as well as a paper mill or two. It's a great city with great people, but man, it can smell pretty bad at times.

I'd been playing youth football since the third grade and was the quarterback or running back on my teams. I was feeling my oats—feeling pretty good about my standing in junior high as a sixth-grader during the spring workouts with the junior high coaches. In Texas, school football starts in the seventh grade, so I was trying to impress the coaches who had already heard about my youth football skills and show them that I was a player.

Well, during these offseason workouts, we held boxing matches for conditioning and competition. I'd been nailin' most of my classmates and wasn't much afraid of anybody. One of my coaches sensed this air of cockiness and complacency and called me over for a visit. I'll never forget how he pumped me up. He was wired up and full of energy. With his veins sticking out of the side of his neck, he said, "James, you badass. See that eighth-grader over there?"

"Yes, sir," I responded.

"I dare you to go over there and tell him you'd rather be dead than a redhead!"

"Yes, sir. You got it!"

So here I am, challenged by a coach I'm trying to impress, and all of my sixth-grade buddies are aware of the dare. I had to do it. I was a little nervous, but just goofy enough to think I could take him. My memory serves me well on this lesson in life. I walked over to this eighth-grader and told him that I'd rather be dead than a redhead.

What followed that pronouncement was a loud "Ooooohhhhh" from the gymnasium where the boxing matches were taking place.

The coaches gave us our gloves to put on, which seemed massive.

We went to our corners.

All the sixth-graders were behind me, and all the-eighth graders were behind "Big Red."

When the coach blew the whistle to start the match, I ran to the middle and started hurling haymakers. A haymaker is a wild swing that comes from the outside and heads toward the supposed victim's ear.

Well, Big Red had a different approach to throwing punches. He had this idea of using straight-ahead jabs, and all I could remember seeing for the next three minutes were these monster-size leather gloves smoking my nose! I had blood flowing from my nose, and there wasn't a thing I could do about it. Big Red was nothing short of Muhammad Ali, and I was his personal punching bag. I got whipped big-time—physically and emotionally.

I tell you this story because it all happened as a result of what we call "fighting words."

So, back to the present and the issue of a playoff system in college football. Following the 2008 season, Utah senator Orrin Hatch came out firing, saying, "The BCS system is anticompetitive, unfair, and in my opinion un-American . . . the system likely violates antitrust law and they'd better fix it or legislation will!"

Senator Hatch is from Utah, and many believe his anger comes from his home state's football team going undefeated in 2008 and not being given a chance to play for the national championship. Utah plays in the Mountain West Conference (MWC); they went 12–0 during the regular season but didn't get a chance to play for the national championship. Instead, as history shows, Florida and Oklahoma—two teams with one loss each—played for the title. And all of you football fans out there saw the whipping Utah put on Alabama in the Sugar Bowl. For all the doubters who didn't believe that the Utes were the real deal, that whooping of the Crimson Tide spoke volumes about how good the Utah program is.

Further proof of unfair treatment to mid-major conference teams is that at the end of the regular season in 2008, three teams in the top eleven were from mid-major conferences. Utah was undefeated and ranked number 6; Boise State was unbeaten and ranked number 9; and TCU had two losses—one to highly ranked Oklahoma and one to fellow MWC rival Utah—and was ranked number 11. Yet only Utah was invited to play in one of the BCS bowls. While Utah was taking care of business against Alabama, TCU and Boise State squared off in the Poinsettia Bowl, and showed the world just how good they both were, playing a game that was decided by only 1 point. The Horned Frogs of TCU outlasted the Broncos of Boise State 17–16.

Having seen those results, it's time for me to play armchair lawyer here and make sure we all understand what Senator Hatch's words mean. Two key points about antitrust laws and what they seek to prevent are:

1. Agreements or practices that restrict free trading and competition between business entities. This includes, in particular, the repression of cartels.
2. Banning abusive behavior by a firm dominating a market, or anticompetitive practices that lead to such a dominant position.

I think it's pretty clear what Senator Hatch was referring to.

In the first definition above, the word "cartel" is used. A cartel is a formal agreement among firms; it is a formal organization of producers that agree to coordinate prices and production. Hang on to those words for a minute, and as I go along, we'll see if what the senator is saying is relevant or not to the major conferences of college football.

Have the major conferences in the past negotiated an agreement among themselves for pricing and revenue sharing, then gone to the TV and radio networks and sponsors to negotiate favorable deals for the production of their product (that is, college football)? Has this caused a splintering effect among college football's other conferences (that is, the mid-majors) whereby they are in a far weaker position to negotiate big rights fees for their conference teams?

Hello, darlin' . . . and hello to some serious fighting words from a U.S. senator. Just as my youthful words received a response in sixth grade, so too will these strong accusations be heard by the architects of the BCS. Can't you just hear the "Ooooohh-hhh" now?

Senator Hatch's statement serves as a spark. His position, along with the existing global economic tsunami, serves as the ignition that will start up the momentum needed for change in the current BCS system.

The Bowl Championship Series consists of the Rose Bowl, the Fiesta Bowl, the Sugar Bowl, and the Orange Bowl. These bowls alternate hosting the title game. The series was created to match the number-1 and number-2 teams in the country at the end of the regular season in the national championship game. This matchup is based on the results of a combination of computer programs and human polls to create a top-25 list. It's hogwash and confusing even to many of us in the business who are paid to understand college football. I hear griping from coaches all the time about the wackiness of having computers help determine who's ranked where.

Furthermore, the polls used in the formula are filled with voters who think they know college football. No doubt there are many qualified voters out there, but many are nothing but former players and coaches who see a couple of games a weekend and watch our Saturday studio shows that give highlights and analyses of the day's games to help them become "qualified" as voters.

I ask you, does watching a thirty-second highlight of a game make you qualified to determine how a certain team played that day?

More times than not, the final score of a game doesn't adequately tell what happened during the entire four quarters of action. Think of how many games you've watched where the score was tight and then the winner hit a couple of late touchdowns to pull away. Or games where a team could have blown out an opponent but the coach decided to back off.

The 2009 Rose Bowl, between USC and Penn State, is a good example. I thought Pete Carroll called the dogs off at halftime with USC up 31–7. Penn State had a nice second half to make the final score a seemingly respectable 38–24 loss. But it wasn't respectable in my eyes. I watched from the sidelines and saw USC overwhelm the Nittany Lions. USC could have won that game 52–14 if they had wanted to. Get my point here? You can't just read scores or watch highlight shows and "know" a team.

I'm going to plant the seed for what I consider to be a viable option for a playoff system. Remember my coach Ron Meyer, who preached KISS: Keep It Simple, Stupid! My goal is to have a system that everybody understands.

Let's cover our bases first with definitions of the conferences. The major conferences are the Big East, the ACC, the SEC, the Big 12, the Big Ten, and the Pac-10. These schools currently have an automatic invitation to the BCS bowls granted to their conference winners.

The mid-major conferences are the MAC, Conference USA, the WAC, and the MWC. I don't want to bog you down with minutiae, but these teams have to go undefeated during the regular season and hope to be ranked high enough to get an invitation to play in one of the BCS bowls.

In my proposed system, at the end of the season, the top eight teams will be invited to the tournament. There's nothing unique to this concept, but the way the eight teams are chosen is different.

The contenders will be the top eight teams determined by our selection committee regardless of conference affiliation. If at the end of the year the selection committee deems that there are four schools out of the SEC who are in the top eight, then so be it; the SEC would have four teams in the tournament. Likewise, if the committee thinks one team from the WAC, one from the MAC, and one from the MWC are in the top eight, then we'll have three schools from the mid-majors in the tournament.

This concept of not guaranteeing a spot to the big six conference winners will no doubt cause significant heartache to the commissioners of the Big East, the ACC, the SEC, the Big 12, the Big Ten, and the Pac-10.

What I've found in my competitive life is that those who do most of the squealing are the ones who are most concerned about not being good enough and are looking for a soft landing or a handout. Hey, if you're good enough, cinch up the pants and get it on! Go recruit great players and coaches and then tell your team's story on the field. Go win games! Quite often I remind those bellyachers that if they want to run with the big dogs, then they need to hike their legs on the tallest tree in the forest.

I like and respect each of those major conferences and think their conference champs are superior to the mid-major conference winners, but that doesn't mean we should rule out the other teams just because they aren't affiliated with a big conference.

Bottom line: if you're feeling offended or uncomfortable with this concept, then you don't have a team or a coach with the ability to be included in the top eight, anyway.

The selection committee will be made up of people who are heavily involved in all conferences—not a beat writer or an analyst from a particular conference. My proposal calls for the people I consider to be the best of the best. I'm talking about the announcers who call the games week in and week out. These friends and colleagues have more knowledge of teams than any group or individuals that I can think of. If I have a serious question or topic I want to ponder regarding college football, the folks I work with will be the ones I go to. We watch hours of film, watch games from coast to coast, know players and coaches, and hear from them what they think of other teams they've faced or seen on TV. College football is in our DNA. We live it.

Of course, there's going to be a push back and reluctance on the part of many factions during this major overhaul. I wouldn't be surprised if the employers of the panel didn't want their announcers/talent/writers on the selection committee. We are journalists and are supposed to report the news, not be the news. But in this particular case, I'd say the networks need to bend on this one for the good of the sport. After all, my colleagues and I have been hired because of our expertise and knowledge of the teams, coaches, and players.

This committee would need to be evaluated annually in order to make sure that each panelist remained in good standing and a major player in the coverage of college football. Part of staying in good standing would be a person-to-person evaluation by the oversight committee to make sure each voter was being fair in their assessment of teams. It is imperative that each voter have zero bias toward a particular conference or team.

To oversee this selection committee, along with me, Commissioner Craig James, I'd ask three highly respected longtime followers of college football to be the initial leaders: Keith Jackson, Brent Musberger, and former Nebraska coach Tom Osborne. In my opinion, you've got four men here who love college football and would be fair in their decision making.

What decisions would we, this oversight committee, make?

Our main role would be to make sure the panel was in place (add or delete panelists as needed), run the committee meetings, and be the spokespersons for the group. When the time came for one of these leaders to move on, the then-standing selection committee would make recommendations for the replacement and a majority vote of a candidate would fill the opening.

Here are some of the types of panelists I'm talking about. (These aren't the only qualified ones, but they will give you a sense of how I'm thinking.)

- **Current ESPN/ABC announcers:** Chris Fowler, Reece Davis, Lee Corso, Kirk Herbstreit, Mark May, Lou Holtz, Andre Ware, Brad Nessler, Todd Blackledge, Ron Franklin, Ed Cunningham, Sean McDonough, Ray Bentley, David Norrie, Rod Gilmore, Bob Griese, Paul Maguire, Bob Davie, John Saunders, Mike Patrick, Trevor Matich, Doug Flutie, and Jesse Palmer
- **Current CBS announcers:** Tim Brando, Spencer Tillman, Verne Lundquist, and Gary Danielson
- **National writers:** Gene Wojciechowski, Bruce Feldman, Pat Forde, Mark Schlabach, Ivan Maisel, Todd McShay, Mel Kiper Jr., Stewart Mandel, and Tony Barnhardt

I like the inclusion of these writers for many reasons, but most important, I like their longtime standing in covering college football. Plus, they aren't restricted to one region or conference because they are national writers.

So what do we do with the existing polls?

I'd leave them alone; let them continue. I've always said that preseason polls are crazy and inexact, yet they start the year off for college football fans by forcing debate on this team and that team, who's good and who's not.

I wouldn't publish or create a weekly poll by our selection committee. Not having any idea how the panel will vote will drive fans (and coaches) crazy! There will be only one poll that matters: the Big One on the Sunday following the last conference championship game. I'm sure fans will know who the top three or four will be, but the final four could present some unbelievable suspense and surprises for teams on the bubble.

My partner John Saunders has said for years how we already have a playoff system in place—that week in and week out, the games mean something. Big John and those of you in his camp: imagine if you were playing to be included in the final eight? We'd have a considerably larger pool of teams playing meaningful games in November. Each and every week would continue to be important. We're just adding to the number of teams down the stretch playing for a shot at the tournament and ultimately a shot at the national championship. What's wrong with that?

Based on my final regular-season ballot, here's how the tournament would have looked:

Final Regular Season Ballot

1. Florida
2. Texas
3. OU
4. Alabama
5. Texas Tech
6. USC
7. Penn State

---

8. Ohio State
9. Utah
10. Cincinnati
11. Oklahoma State
12. Georgia Tech
13. Boise State
14. Oregon
15. TCU
16. Georgia
17. Northwestern
18. Michigan State
19. Mississippi
20. Pittsburgh
21. Missouri
22. Oregon State
23. Virginia Tech
24. Brigham Young
25. West Virginia

What happens to the bowl games as we've known them?

As of the 2008 bowl season, there were plenty of them—thirty-four to be exact. That's 68 teams playing in a bowl game out of 119 in Division 1A. I have no problem with there being a ton of bowl games. They are a reward for many schools and players. Consider the programs out there that haven't been to a bowl game in years, and how important that last weekend is to those bubble teams looking to earn that sixth win to become bowl-eligible. How cool was it to watch Vanderbilt beat Kentucky in the middle of November 2008 to become bowl-eligible for the first time since 1982?

I think a far greater concern for most bowl games will be whether or not they survive this economic tsunami. As Americans, we've been drilled for months now about cutbacks, layoffs, and reduced spending on advertising. My guess is that there will be some bowl games that don't survive this economy.

As for my mythical playoff, the opening round of the "tournament" would be played in the Rose (Pasadena), Sugar (New Orleans), Fiesta (Glendale, Arizona), and Orange (Miami) bowls.

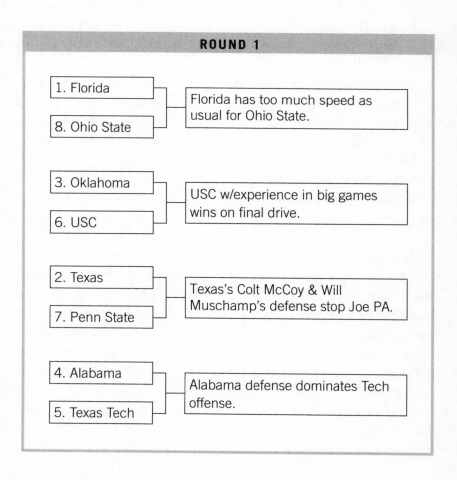

ROUND 1

1. Florida
8. Ohio State
Florida has too much speed as usual for Ohio State.

3. Oklahoma
6. USC
USC w/experience in big games wins on final drive.

2. Texas
7. Penn State
Texas's Colt McCoy & Will Muschamp's defense stop Joe PA.

4. Alabama
5. Texas Tech
Alabama defense dominates Tech offense.

The first games would be played the weekend *before* the traditional New Year's Day games, so that round two would occur on or about New Year's and the championship game would be played a week after all the other games have been played.

Something to keep in mind is that I feel good about the chances for this move because of the political pressure for change as well as an economy that is forcing *all* industries to change. With that in mind, let's open the floor for bidding by any city or bowl interested in getting into the mix of hosting a tournament game. If Orlando or San Antonio or Tampa or San Diego wants to step up and buy their way in, they should be able to do it.

For those saying this has no chance at all of happening, raise your hand if you ever thought that our federal government would be financially bailing out American businesses. The world has changed big-time! If our country's banking and automobile industries can be totally revamped overnight, then so, too, can the structure of college football.

Round two could alternate between the four bowls that win the rights to host them. The two bowls not hosting a game during their off year in the second round would be able to have an additional game to fill their traditional slot. For example, let's say in year one that the Rose Bowl and the Orange Bowl are hosting round-two games. That means the Fiesta and Sugar bowls wouldn't have a round-two game, but they could invite other nontournament teams to their sites for that date so they can keep their traditions alive. The two off years by these bowls would help fill the void for any bowls that might not survive this economic meltdown.

The championship game would be played each year in Jerry Jones's brand-new state-of-the-art massive enclosed stadium. The Dallas Cowboys' stadium is centrally located in Dallas/Fort

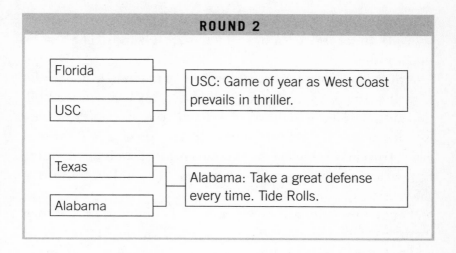

Worth and offers protection from bad weather. I know Jerry and believe in him and his ability to go out and bid to get this annual jewel. It would be good for the new Cowboys stadium and for fans, too. There isn't a venue in America as nice as this stadium. Everybody would win in this setting.

If college football wants to keep all 119 Division 1A schools viable and maintain the depth of love for the sport as we know it, then some form of revenue sharing will have to occur.

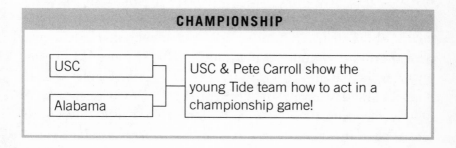

Understand that only fifteen to twenty athletic departments are able to either break even or make money. That's it. The rest are under water.

Any way you look at it, college football is a billion-dollar-plus annual business. Over the last six years there's been nearly a billion dollars paid out in bowl games alone. But most of the money is going to the big schools—schools that are in a BCS conference. The crazy thing is that the mid-major schools are trying to compete in every sense with the majors, with only a fraction of the revenue.

I'm told the SEC will distribute $11.1 million to each of their members from TV- and radio-rights fees. That doesn't include an additional $11.6 million for schools that participated in bowls. On the other end of the spectrum, Conference USA will distribute $2 million in rights fees to their members. Conference USA isn't in their boat alone—the WAC, the MAC, and the MWC have the same budget issues.

In order for these mid-majors to continue to compete on the field and to have enough glitz in their facilities, the universities have had to step in with money from their schools' resources. These subsidies for athletic departments are taking money from the schools' ability to pay professors and to award scholarship money to top-flight students.

Talk about subsidizing—SMU is a prime example of a member of Conference USA that had to step up financially in order to get their new coach, June Jones. Jones had a reputation as a coach who had taken another mid-major school, Hawaii, and turned around its football program. In 2007, Jones led Hawaii on a remarkable run, going undefeated during the regular season. The Rainbow Warriors then accepted a bid to play in a BCS bowl game against the Georgia Bulldogs. The 2008 Sugar Bowl had a lot of intrigue because Hawaii had a great regular season, so the comparisons to the major conferences were inevitable. But Georgia took it upon themselves to make sure little ol' Hawaii left knowing what it was like to play against an SEC team. UGA smoked Hawaii, 41–10.

So here was Jones, making a reported $800,000 at Hawaii, and SMU wanted him. Hawaii had upped their offer for Jones to a reported $1.7 million; SMU didn't flinch and at least matched it. Many reports have the total package at nearly $2 million a year. Think about it: SMU had to offer Jones about as much as their entire annual football budget. In order to make the offer, athletic director Steve Orsini hit the streets hard, personally calling on the top money men and women of SMU. Orsini had to get the approval and money commitments before he could solidify the deal with Jones. This all took place at the end of 2007, well before the economy went in the tank. Orsini got it done, and Jones was hired as the new football coach of SMU.

SMU is the poster child for mid-major conference teams trying to run with the big dogs. High school kids are looking to attend a college that provides well-rounded experience. They want to be able to cheer for their team on Saturdays. My daughter Jessica graduated from SMU in 2006. Jessica loved SMU, but like most of her friends, she had to adopt another football team to cheer for because SMU was terrible. Time will tell if Jones was worth the investment.

Is it worth paying these coaches a million or more dollars a year? Here are some more data that will make you stop and scratch your head in amazement.

Texas Tech hired Mike Leach as their head coach for the 2000 season. Entering the 2008 season, Leach had taken his teams to a bowl game all eight seasons. Tech's chancellor, Kent Hance, said that when Tech entered the Big 12 South division in 1996, the school had an endowment of $50 million. Since then, the endowment has grown to nearly $700 million. Over the last ten years, Tech has spent $200 million on sports facilities alone. No way that would have happened if Tech hadn't been competitive and winning football games. The school's enrollment and interest from around the country have picked up significantly. It's not just because of Leach and his staff; Tech's athletic department has done a great job of engaging their fan base. That fan base has created an atmosphere that allowed Leach and his staff to recruit top-shelf players. I'd say the investment by all involved at Tech has been well worth it.

We need to take the BCS bowl game money and appropriately reward the schools that are playing in the tournament, and then split the rest of the money evenly with the other teams in Division 1A.

That would curtail the need for all of these schools to be out running around raising money all the time. It would also take the burden off these schools' administrations that have to foot the losses of their athletic departments. Obviously, the academicians would appreciate this. For years, as long as I can remember, athletic departments have been able to call on big-wallet boosters to help them offset shortfalls in money. But with this economy as it is, those boosters either don't have any money to give or they are sitting tight trying to hang on themselves. I'm telling you, this economy is going to be a significant nail in the coffin for many schools.

I've recently read that even big schools like Stanford and Ohio State are feeling the crunch. Stanford and Ohio State have huge endowments, and in the past, plenty of boosters would fill the voids. Stanford has mentioned that they are considering having to drop some sports programs in order to have enough money to sustain the remaining sports.

I believe that there's additional money out there to be had by college sports. As always, football is the water that floats the ships of athletic departments. Outside of basketball, most sports are financial drains on the budget. Yet, college sports is the second-largest sports industry after the NFL.

How does this information sit with you? The NFL and the NBA combined receive twenty times the amount of money for TV and radio rights compared to college sports. Twenty times! But the NFL and the NBA only have two times the viewers of college sports. That's a big gap. There's money left on the table for college sports. But has the cartel-type environment of the major conferences truly weakened the amount of money that might be out there?

At the end of the day, college football is at an all-time high in popularity. TV ratings are up as well as game-day attendance. I believe we're about to enter a phase in college football that really accentuates the haves and have-nots. We're heading for a sport where you've got the top thirty programs being able to compete and the rest of the country relegated to inferiority in all areas. I know you've heard the saying that a chain is only as strong as its weakest link. Fans are loving the game as it is today. Cinderella has a chance every Saturday to provide a great upset. With this economy being as down as it is, we're going to see a dramatic drop-off in athletic departments' abilities to patch or raise the extra dollars needed to stay competitive.

My friend and former Patriots teammate Guy Morriss used to call one of his Baylor boosters for extra jack all the time. Guy would call and ask for $10,000 so he could buy a new sled for his team. No problem . . . in the old economy. Not today. No way these coaches and athletic directors will be able to bandage their budget shortfalls.

The perfect storm is in place for the change I've suggested. Sure, we will come out of this economic challenge, but as of today, businesses in every sector have been impacted and therefore are forced to evaluate the way they conduct business. College football is no different. Fans have been calling for a change for years. The consumer wants a champion determined *on the field*. Even newly elected President Barack Obama has openly stated his support for an eight-team playoff. While I disagree with many of his other views, I applaud his stance on a playoff system. The man's swinging a stick that's made changes to our government like never before. In today's world, expect the unexpected!

YOU'RE ONLY AS GOOD AS YOUR LAST RECRUITING CLASS

In chapter 5 I told you how important recruiting is to a coach's success. There's just no way around it: you've got to have the talent in order to win. If you were to ask me what's changed the most in college football over the last twenty-five years, I'd say, hands down, it's recruiting. The rules of what a coach can say and do have changed tremendously, in part due to the crazy things that were taking place during the 1970s and early 1980s. The NCAA has corralled the Wild West ways of coaches and boosters and evened the playing field for the smaller-budget schools by enacting a strict set of guidelines to cover all aspects of recruiting.

Bear with me as I take you on a journey back to the wild days, so you'll better appreciate or understand how much recruiting has changed.

Being nicknamed "the Pony" can be both good and bad. I always appreciate and feel honored when somebody comes up and says nice things about Eric Dickerson and me, the Pony Express—about how good we were and all that stuff. But as I've learned over the years, you've got to take the good along with the bad.

Wherever I go, it's almost a given that somebody's going to shout out something about SMU and the old recruiting days. "Hey, Pony . . . must have been pretty good in the old days. I imagine those annuities you got are starting to kick in!" Or I'll get these jewels: "Best team money could buy!" "What's it like to have to pay taxes now?" "Who made more? You or Dickerson?"

My standard reaction is to go along with the jabs—it would do me no good to try and defend all the crazy stories that emerged from the old days. But for here and now, I'll answer the above questions: I had an awesome experience at SMU; there are no annuities on my behalf (if I'd known what they were maybe I'd have asked for one!); paying taxes isn't fun; and playing with Eric Dickerson was a pleasure.

To say it was wild during my recruiting year of 1978 would be a significant understatement. I was the Texas high school player of the year and had broken the all-time rushing record, so I was being recruited by everybody. Even head coach Barry Switzer of the Oklahoma Sooners wanted me. I'm laughing as I write this because Coach Switzer and I recently had a conversation, and he was telling me that people ask him if he ever recruited a white running back. Coach flatters me by saying only one—Craig James! And they say, "Oh, okay." Coach tells 'em that, other than me, he was looking for the Dickersons or Earl Campbells or Billy Sims of the world. I tell you this so you understand that I was heavily recruited and was well aware of the "deals" going on at that time.

I'm not going to mention any names of coaches or schools because it's water under the bridge, and it wouldn't be fair to the people or the universities if I used their names.

The NCAA didn't just wake up in 2008 and establish rules to live by while recruiting. The changes that have been implemented over time have been done for the good of both coaches and players. Coaches used to be on the road all the time trying to keep up with their competitors. A coach didn't want to take the chance that his target athlete was being courted by some other school. Therefore, not only was the coach spending time and money on the road, the young athlete was being hounded by these recruiters all the time.

On the one hand, these countless encounters between coach and player were great. It gave both parties a chance to really get to know each other. However, I'm reminded of the hound dog hangin' around the chicken coop as a guard for the coyotes. All of a sudden that chicken looks pretty good, know what I mean? Well, too many dates between a coach and a player allowed more opportunities for that coach to break the rules. The NCAA's decision over time to limit the number of days a coach can be on the road has greatly helped everybody involved. Plus, limiting the number of times a coach can personally see a kid is good, too.

Remember now that I had committed to SMU before my senior season of high school had even started. At that time I was considered a blue-chipper—someone who had a lot of potential. I'd been All District as a junior and had good size and speed. I was listed at 6 foot 1 and weighed about 210 pounds, but I hadn't broken out yet as a player in a big way. Unlike today, in 1978, there weren't Internet or recruiting services or any kind of organizations in the business of promoting players. Back then you could make a commitment to the school after your junior season, but most pledges by players didn't happen until after they'd taken their official visits. And those visits didn't happen until after your senior football season was over.

I committed to SMU early because my girlfriend (now my wife), Marilyn, was a year ahead of me and going to SMU. But my early commitment didn't stop the other schools around the country from trying to get me to change my mind.

My first indication that recruiting was going to be interesting was around the first part of my senior season. My buddies and I had gone to our favorite local Mexican restaurant. We were pretty regular customers at La Hacienda. Well, this one particular night we'd finished eating and this man comes up to our table and introduces himself as coach *blah-blah* (he wasn't from SMU). He was a very nice man, and seemed even nicer when he asked for our check. This coach had heard that I liked La Hacienda and was a regular there, so he made himself a regular there, too. After about six games, I'd already passed a thousand yards, and from that point on, my buddies and I didn't have to worry about paying for dinner too often.

It was a weird dynamic back then compared to today. Nowadays coaches are limited to the number of times they can actually see a recruit. The rules change frequently about how many times contact can be made, but it's a few times at the most. Heck, in 1978 it seemed like I was seeing coaches all the time. It was kind of cool, though, because I really got to know a coach. We didn't have cell phones or e-mail, so personal interaction was the way it happened. With today's restrictions, how could either coach or player really get to know each other?

There were five or six of my high school teammates being recruited, too, so Stratford High School was a must stop on the recruiting circuit. We were good kids, but as a group, like most high school seniors, we were capable of having our moments.

There was a coach who'd set up a visit with my buddies and me one afternoon. This coach came in from the Midwest and was a good guy. He'd played in the NFL, and that impressed the heck out of us. So we agreed to meet him after school at the local pizza parlor. It cracks me up now thinking about it, but we met the coach in the middle of the afternoon off campus to talk about his school and to get to know him better. Well, this coach liked his beer, and he personally pounded a couple of pitchers. We didn't partake in the consumption, but here we were sitting there wondering what in the world this coach was thinking. We were kicking one another under the table and having a blast.

The next day the coach came by the school, and I got called out of class to go down to the coaches' office to meet with this wild man from the Midwest. "Hello, Coach . . . how are you?"

"Great, Craig, thanks for coming down."

It was a one-on-one conversation, and the first time in my life I was stumped as to how to reply to a person. Here was the coach's offer: if I came to his school, I'd get a condominium for my family, they'd fly my family up for all games, and I'd get $1,000 a month. I was one wide-eyed eighteen-year-old!

When the conversation started, he was sober and so was I. But after his offer, I really wanted to ask him if we could go back to the pizza joint so we could both drink beer. Back then, for those of you keeping score, the legal drinking age was eighteen.

To put a nice bow around the "street business" of that recruiting era, here are the parameters of what kind of deals were out there:

- For a really good blue-chipper—a top-shelf player guaranteed to play his freshman year and a real difference-maker: a car, an up-front cash payment of $50,000, and a monthly allowance of $1,000. I'm sure a lot of you are shaking your heads at this, saying, "Wow! What was the NCAA thinking?" Obviously, the NCAA didn't allow this and was trying as best they could to police schools around the country. There wasn't a snowball's chance in hell they could monitor each school and their boosters.
- For a pretty good player who letters four years: a little cash up front and a couple of hundred bucks a month.
- For a run-of-the-mill guy: a slap on the shoulder and a solid, "Atta boy . . . Work hard, son!"

Crazy, isn't it? Even as I write this, I'm shaking my head in bewilderment. But it was what it was. Times sure have changed.

Now that I've exposed some of the things I knew were going on, let me give you something to consider. Coaches are competitive people who want to win. And back in the day, they were doing nothing unique when on the road, doing what they had to do to get a kid to sign with their school. I'd be remiss if I didn't say that not all coaches were out on the road bending the rules. Notice that I say "bending"? Try to place yourself in their shoes at that place in time to maybe better understand why they did what they did.

As for the player/recruit, think back to when you were seventeen or eighteen years old. What would you have done if you were offered something you'd never dreamed of having? Most young men, me included, had never had any luxuries in their lives. I never went to bed hungry nor did I ever not have shoes or clothes to go to school in, but I guarantee you I didn't live high on the hog, spending a thousand dollars a month! I remember my stepdad Charlie looking me dead in the face after one crazy offer like, Son, damn, that's a lot of money!

Still working my way through the years and heading to the present, it wasn't always about moolah! There were plenty of funny stories and fond memories to last a lifetime.

Throughout the years, I've come to realize that I'm a bit of a pack rat. I just can't seem to get up the nerve to throw stuff away. I keep thinking that when I get older, I'll need all of these articles and photos to help stroke my bruised ego—and I'll have loads of boxes to sift through.

At any rate, recently I was in the attic, sweating my fanny off and reading my old clippings. And besides making myself feel good, it struck me that certain aspects of the recruiting game really haven't changed all that much. When you break it down, recruiting will always be a process whereby schools sell parents on how much they have to offer a young student-athlete. And

I was amazed at all of the correspondence that I had received during the recruiting process. It was—and still is—all about *communication*.

But the way that schools get material out and stay in touch with players today versus twenty-five years ago has changed drastically. Back then, it was delivered by the good old U.S. Postal Service. Letters upon letters were sent to me and my fellow teammates. I remember my mother telling me one day that I'd received a big box from the postman. I opened it and it was full of letters from people at the University of Arkansas, hundreds of them. Apparently the Arkansas coaches had given their fans and alumni the wrong mailing address for my family, so instead of my getting a bunch of letters spread out over the course of a year, I got one big box filled with them. Their tardiness served them better than if they had actually been delivered on time. I was impressed by the sheer number of letters in one box. (And yeah, I can hear all you wise guys out there crackin' about how Arkansas messed up and that SMU recruits were used to getting boxes all right—boxes full of green paper with Benjamin Franklin's picture on them.)

Riffling through the letters, I found these yellow pieces of paper. They were Western Union telegrams. That'll date me, since most kids today have no idea what a telegram is. I had ones from Bob Hope, John Wayne's doctor (not the Duke himself, but still impressive, I thought), Aaron Spelling, and dozens more. Hollywood names and stars were sending me notes. I couldn't believe it. Pretty impressive form of marketing by schools!

How many have heard the old saying "Money talks and bull—walks"? Back in the day there were a few different ways to get a player. Some schools got lucky, and a kid was perfectly content to play for a free education. Others needed enticements (ahhh, moolah!). But then there was the old-fashioned way of just plain hard recruiting, convincing the kid that it would be his honor to play for a school.

Easily the highlight of my recruiting came from the Big Dog himself—Alabama coach Paul "Bear" Bryant.

Hands down, the most impressive person I encountered during recruiting was Coach Bryant. When Coach Bryant would call me on the phone, I used to freeze up. His old gravelly, growling, raspy voice was unmistakable and intimidating as heck. I'll never forget the first time the Alabama coaches made contact with me. My teammates and I had just won the Texas AAAA state championship. I was walking off the field in the Houston Astrodome, and this man came up and introduced himself as the running backs coach at Alabama.

"Wow. Nice to meet you, sir!" I said.

That encounter was followed up with Coach Bryant's personal invitation for me to come to Tuscaloosa to visit the Tide.

As I've mentioned, my high school team was the best team I ever played on. Apples to apples, we were better than my college conference championship teams and even better than my Super Bowl New England Patriots team. We were 15–0 and dominated the state of Texas. I rushed for 2,411 yards and had 35 TDs my senior year, which broke the single-season rushing mark in Texas.

My high school team ran the wishbone, and I was the left halfback. Alabama ran the wishbone and was looking for a left halfback. Here I was, a white kid in Texas, breaking the rushing record—Coach Bryant later would tell me he had real doubts about some white kid breaking the Texas rushing record and scratched his head wondering if I was for real.

Let me tell you about Coach Bryant. He quickly figured out that the only way he was going to get me to Alabama was if he could get my high school sweetheart to transfer there. My girlfriend was a year older than I was and she was already a freshman at SMU. That's why I had committed early to the Mustangs. For those out there thinking that I needed to take a urine test for committing to SMU and not immediately going with 'Bama, I agree that it seems a little wacky! Puppy love was whippin' my young fanny. How many times do young high school sweethearts follow each other to college only to get there and realize there are other fish in the pond?

I was lucky, and it worked out. I was also lucky that SMU's record improved. When I was in junior high, my buddies and I used to tease each other and say that if you didn't get any better you'd have to play at Shmoo (SMU). They'd been pretty bad for a long time. Quite honestly, at the time I committed to Coach Meyer, I didn't think I was good enough to play anywhere else. Everybody kept telling me I should go to the University of Texas. I was like, "No way!"

I grew up watching and rooting for the Horns when Darrell Royal was the coach. The Horns were bigger than big. I knew Shmoo was a place I had a chance to play at.

Fast-forward a couple of weeks to my recruiting trip to 'Bama. The first students I met were my host and hostess for the weekend. The host was an offensive lineman on the team. The hostess was what they called a Bears Angel. And she was an angel—a beautiful and sweet person who seemed so interested in helping me make up my mind about which school I should attend (hint: it wasn't SMU). I had a great time with my escorts, and I went home semi-confused. I still knew that I was going to school wherever my girlfriend was, but now I thought that maybe she should start thinking about transferring to Alabama.

During my exit visit with Coach Bryant in his office, he was smoking cigarettes and the room was filled with smoke. Imagine that happening today! I'm sitting across from Coach and I bet I didn't sleep thirty minutes the night before. The Tide players all lived in one dorm, and this dorm had guest rooms for recruits to stay in. I initially got back to my room around three in the morning. I got in bed, and the next thing I hear is this massive howling going on in the hallway. A few of the Alabama players came in feeling pretty good . . . and decided to have a wrestling match.

These big guys were throwing one another all over the place. I was scared to death they were going to call me out to join in the brawl. Hey, I was already on edge from my visit over at former Alabama All-American Bob Baumhauer's house. The big man was at that time a player for the Miami Dolphins, and he had legs as wide as his truck. The reason we went to his house was so he could show me his pet lion cub! Yeah, no kidding—a pet lion cub named Oscar.

So the next morning in my exit interview with Coach Bryant, he looked across his desk and said to me, "Boy, you and your mama know where you want to go to school." Man, he was intimidating as hell. Then he went on to say that he wasn't giving up and that he'd be in touch.

I think I slept an entire week when I got home from Alabama.

True to his word, about two weeks later I was returning home to Houston from my weekend visit to Dallas and SMU's campus, seeing my girlfriend. Now, this was back when cell phones weren't even a thought, so I had no idea that I had a guest waiting for me upon my return. (For the record, I did have a CB in my car—citizens' band radio, in case you're wondering. My handle was "Silver Bullet." But no one contacted me on the CB to let me know what was up.) So I walked into our apartment in Houston and there she was—the Bears Angel hostess from Alabama. Man, I suddenly realized that the game was on. Coach Bryant meant business, and he was on a mission to either get my girlfriend to transfer or to see if he could put a little wedge between me and my best gal.

Coach Bryant then went on a tear, calling my girlfriend's parents and asking them to help with the situation—to see if they could get their daughter to transfer. Then he hit me up, telling me, "Boy, we'll make her a Bears Angel; that'll get her a little spendin' money. Know what I mean?"

I was thinking, *No way is my girlfriend showing any recruits around!*

Well, it is well documented: I decided to stick with my commitment to SMU and my girlfriend. Telling Coach Bryant I wasn't going to attend Alabama was very hard to do. But it ended up being the right decision. My girlfriend and I dated seven years before being married in 1983. We recently celebrated our twenty-fifth anniversary, with four kids to boot.

Also for the record, I did not go to SMU because of any monetary enticements! I was following my girlfriend and that is it—period!! Now, I'm not going to sit here and tell you I never received a nickel during my playing days. But I can say with certainty that no benefits were ever extended to me from anyone associated with the SMU administration. I also want to say that the few men who took the heat for the downfall of SMU are not bad men! They loved SMU! And for many years their involvement made almost all SMU alums beam with pride and happiness. I'm not defending their actions, but I am defending their hearts.

Perhaps the thing that irks me the most about getting ribbed by people about SMU's recruiting practices is that what was happening at SMU was happening all over the country. I just gave you a few of the many examples from schools that weren't in the old SWC. The fact that it was going on everywhere didn't make it right, nor was what SMU was doing right.

Nor, for that matter, was the "death penalty" right for SMU. The NCAA had no idea how dramatic and lasting an impact it would have on a school. To the best of my knowledge, only a few individuals were found to have been continuing illegal benefits to a handful of players. The handing down of the death penalty went well beyond penalizing a few culprits. It has stained and tarnished a tremendous institution and all of its graduates for far too long. I sit here today and it's easy to second-guess the NCAA's decision to halt play at SMU for the 1987 season—SMU also added its own additional season of not playing football, so the school didn't play games for two complete seasons. The ultimate downside to this was that SMU's weakness kept them from being included when the Southwest Conference broke up. Texas, Texas A&M, Texas Tech, and Baylor were invited/included in the expansion of the Big 8. SMU not being in the Big 12 has kept them from recruiting on the same level as other major conference schools.

It's so easy to look at things with hindsight and pass judgment. It's not fair or right to do that without really placing yourself back in that environment and time. It's like when I look back on my decision to leave *College GameDay*. Today I think, no way should I have done that. But when I put myself back in that moment and recall the hardship it was placing on my family, the decision to leave was the appropriate thing to do.

That was then . . . this is now.

I want to take the time to offer up advice to parents and/or players who might one day go through recruiting. Since I just went through it as a parent with both of my boys, I hope these thoughts help if you ever have to deal with recruiting.

When making big decisions I try to know as much as possible about the people or subject I'm considering. As for recruiting, it's important to know that coaches are normal people. Some are smart, some are dumb; some are high-strung, some are laid-back.

These guys work hard and are on the road away from their families a lot. So it should be no surprise to know that they have fun . . . when possible. Here's what I mean.

As far as I know, there aren't any pizza parlor meetings or beer sessions with recruits anymore. Coaches have to be a lot more discreet and guarded. The coaching fraternity is pretty close-knit. Many times in Dallas during recruiting season, I'll get a call from Bret Bielema, head coach of Wisconsin, or Mark Stoops, defensive coordinator at Arizona, saying the gang is in town and meeting for dinner somewhere at nine o'clock, usually at Del Frisco's steak house.

The gang is a hodgepodge of coaches from all different schools. Many times these coaches are in town trying to get a verbal commitment from the same kid. This late-night, out-of-town hangin' has been going on a long time. When everybody gets to dinner at Del Frisco's, all competition is out the window and it's just good fellowship—coaches catching up with old buddies or perhaps reminiscing about times when they used to coach together.

And as boys will do, there's the butt-busting that takes place! Like the time Mark Stoops—brother of Bob of OU fame and Mike, who is head coach at Arizona and Mark's boss—thought he'd lost his new black leather jacket. Stoops had gotten up from the table and was making the rounds, shooting the breeze; he'd had his nice cigar and glass of wine and it was time to go. Well, the lights were dimly lit and he couldn't see that his jacket was still draped over the chair he'd been sitting in. Stoops was fired up! Of course, Bielema and I didn't help the situation at all. We saw his jacket and knew where it was. So we started jackin' him, saying, "Hey, Mark, I think I saw this man walk out with it on." Stoops went charging around looking for the dude. He was ready to head-butt somebody. We laughed our fannies off; you'd have thought Stoops had a million dollars in that jacket! When he finally found the jacket, he obviously called us a bunch of idiots. (That's the clean version of what he said to us.)

What I'm trying to say is that coaches are people just like me and you. At the end of the day, respect them, but don't get goofy and stumble all over them. Parents who do that are the ones who are trying hard to sell their kids—and more than likely their kids aren't up to the next level's standards. These coaches have to find players who can help them win games. If your son is good, they're going to offer him a scholarship or an invitation to walk on to their team. If he doesn't fit their school's plans, all that butt-kissing isn't going to help. As a matter of fact, most coaches are turned off by parents who work them. Again, be respectful and ask questions, but spend your time with them trying to get to know their schools' plans for your son.

In chapter 6 I mentioned my friend and Penn State defensive back coordinator Tom Bradley saying that recruiting is an inexact science. Here's what he means: coaches have a tough task trying to evaluate a young man who is seventeen or eighteen years old. They have to project what that kid will be like two years down the road. Has the kid already peaked? Is he a good student/ citizen? Will he fit into the culture of their team's locker room? Are his parents idiots or (a nicer way of saying it) are they unrealistic about their kid's ability?

Go to your favorite schools' summer camps. I think this is perhaps the most important thing I can suggest you do. No doubt, summer camps for schools are a way for coaches to make extra money. But it's also a way for coaches to get to know a prospective player. Preferably, for both the kid and the school, the youngster starts going to camps the summer before his junior year. In many ways I totally disagree with this entire concept of kids thinking they are being "recruited" by a school so early. It only feeds the fire at home by some moms and dads who continue to believe their little Johnny is the next Heisman Trophy winner. You know the kind of parent I'm talking about—go to any youth ball field in the country and you'll see four or five delusional parents per team.

Only one time in my life do I remember a parent being right about his kid's future. I was in San Antonio, for the U.S. Army All-American game. I was in the hotel gym, and this dad came up and introduced himself. He went on and on about his son trying to decide between this school and that, but he was going to go to Florida to play QB for the Gators. I thought this dad was the typical goof ball! Boy, was I wrong. My gym rat buddy that day was Bob Tebow, the father of Heisman stud Tim!

The reason I recommend these camps is simple. At these camps, coaches are pretty much uncensored by the NCAA rules, allowing them to chat as much as they please with a "camper." Back to what Coach Bradley said about recruiting being an inexact science: the more a coach knows a kid, the better chance both parties have of making a good decision—for the kid, where to go to school; for the coach, whether or not the young man can fit in at his school.

Again, experience with my boys supports my conviction about the importance of summer camps. Neither Adam nor Andy was a summer camper. Adam was a baseball player and had no time to go to camps. Andy was going to a couple of camps his junior summer, but his high school seven-on-seven passing league team was playing in the state championships during the times that the camps he was interested in were being held. Did it hurt them? Absolutely. Coaches didn't get a chance to see their bodies, their personalities, or their skills.

Adam did go to the U.S. Army All-American day camp following his junior year. This was a crazy experience. The rumor was that it was an invitation camp only. What I found was that you could get an invitation as long as you paid the several-hundred-dollar camper's fee! Still, for the most part, there were a lot of really talented players there from all over the country. Fundamentally, the camp's idea of gathering 40-yard times, 20-yard shuttle times, agility exercises, and skills work was a great plan. All of these drills were videotaped, so a player left with a great marketing tape. That was Adam's post-junior season.

I'm different from a lot of parents or dads in that I've made a living either playing the game or covering it. Therefore, I know how to evaluate a player. My assessment of Adam after his junior year was that he had great feet, above-average speed, and excellent hands. That was his strength—great receiving ability. Adam was 6 feet 2 inches and about 230 pounds. I thought he'd be a perfect hybrid tight end/receiver—meaning he was big enough to line up tight and block or to get out wide in a slot and run routes.

Now, fast-forward to his senior season. The U.S. Army selection committee sent out a request to all previous junior campers for an updated game tape. I have a nice digital video camera that I use to record my kids playing sports. If you see me at one of my kids' games, you'll see me with my camera going full-tilt on every play. So I sat down and edited an updated highlight tape of Adam and sent it off to the selection committee. The tape had probably four or five games of him playing. It was enough to show him catching the ball and blocking and his overall skills as a player. Don't make a tape that's an hour long! Pick out ten plays or so that shows your kid making plays running around the field. Coaches don't have time to sit through your kid's highlight tape.

A couple of weeks later, Adam got a call from the U.S. Army committee informing him he'd been selected to play in their game. Needless to say, he was honored and fired up.

There's no doubt in Adam's mind or mine that if he hadn't gone to their camp, and eventually gotten invited to play in their game, he would have had a much harder time getting a scholarship to Texas Tech. The Army All-American game allowed Adam a platform to showcase his ability against other players from around the country. It all started with him going to a camp.

My other son, Andy, didn't go to a summer camp because of timing conflicts. Therefore, Andy wasn't on the radar of these schools. Plus, while he did play on varsity as a junior, he was a late bloomer and started coming on strong as his senior year started, becoming an All-State tight end. I remember sitting down to edit his tapes for a highlight tape to send off and watching from a football standpoint how much he had improved week to week. That's great for his team and for his own personal confidence. But with colleges earmarking and offering kids as juniors, Andy not being on their watch list from previous summer camps put him at a decided disadvantage. It drives me crazy as a football guy and without rose-colored glasses (daddy ball), to sit and watch Andy play and know that he's better than a lot of the kids already committed to schools he's interested in. If Andy chooses to play, the beautiful thing about him is that he wants to go to a college that he knows he wants to attend and get a great education.

One of the schools he was interested in was the University of Colorado. I called Coach Dan Hawkins and told him about Andy. Dan's a smart guy and immediately said, "Yes, I'm interested. Get me a tape so we can look at him." I called Dan in late December, so by that time he'd already filled up his scholarships for the recruiting class. As a general rule, schools have twenty-five scholarships to give out a year. I knew this before I called and inquired, but not getting a scholarship with it being so late in the recruiting season didn't bother us. We were looking for the right fit for Andy, should he decide he wanted to play football in college.

As of the writing of this book, Andy was going to visit Colorado and he'd already visited Texas Tech. Andy had narrowed his thinking down to those two schools and was being recruited as a preferred walk-on. That status allows a school to add more players to a recruiting class, usually around five or so, who will have to pay their tuition but are treated the same as all the other athletes. I admire Dan Hawkins for seeing Andy's tape and recognizing a 6-foot-2, 190-pound kid who can run and play. Dan also was smart enough to know that Andy had good blood—meaning his dad played in the NFL, his uncle Chris played ten years of major league baseball, and his older brother, Adam, was a player at Texas Tech. I throw props to Dan because not all coaches are able to understand that and see outside the box. Remember what I said earlier about coaches? Some are smart, some are dumb.

Put a highlight tape together of your son/player! I just told you how big a deal putting together Adam's tape was for him. No doubt it was important for Andy, too. It's critical that you immediately understand that you must learn how to market your son to schools. It's also important to know that just because your son is getting a "recruiting" letter from a school doesn't mean you are being recruited. All that letter means is that the coach has somehow been told that you might be a player. You're a prospect in the sense that at least you are on that school's radar. Hey, it's better than not getting a letter, but don't assume that a coach even knows you've been getting letters from his school. That school's recruiting coordinator might know who you are, but the position coach might not. This highlight tape needs to get to the recruiting coordinator as soon as possible. I'd send in a junior-year tape so they can at least begin to analyze the athlete.

As for being aggressive, when I was at the U.S. Army All-American game, I had parents come up to me with tapes of their kids asking me to evaluate them. While I laughed at this process, I deep down inside admired them for being aggressive and trying to help their sons get attention.

Being real now, Bob Tebow didn't need to give me a tape of Tim. Tim was a no-brainer decision for any school. But not everybody is a Tim Tebow–type talent; most aren't, and they need to get in front of these coaches.

Here's a suggestion for you athletes: the only things you can control as a player are your attitude and your effort. Knowing how hard it is to get a scholarship, try as best as you can to work hard to prepare yourself to maximize the talent you have. Enjoy your friends and your senior season. My high school coach always told me that the cream will rise to the top. For you butter churners out there, that means you keep grinding away and eventually the good stuff will rise. For you players it means that if you've got talent, it will work out. I told you earlier how my ESPN friend said that chance favors a prepared mind. Well, the same thing goes with sports. If you work hard, you'll give yourself the best shot possible at obtaining your dream.

In summary, recruiting has changed significantly from the days of buying guys. You and I would both be naive to think that cheating and payments don't still occur. There's no way you'll ever be able to monitor the actions of every school's boosters. I do have a stern recommendation for the NCAA: promote and make sure that each and every player and coach in college athletics signs an agreement that is simple to read and says that if a player gets caught taking illegal benefits, that player will lose considerable playing time. I'm being lenient with the player because these guys are young and don't fully understand the consequences of accepting something, or that playing time would start with a minimum of a half year of eligibility for the first violation and increase to a full year if caught again.

I'd nail the coach caught cheating. These are grown men who fully understand the rules and consequences. If caught and convicted, these offenders would be suspended from coaching in the NCAA for two years. Stiff? Yes, but only an idiot would cheat knowing he was risking his job and, more than likely, his career as a result of his actions.

YOU CAN'T
TEACH TALENT

ollege football means a lot of things to a lot of people. I'm drawn to the sport because of the passion displayed by the players week in and week out, the traditions that are honored year in and year out, and the freshness and new beginning each year brings.

The uncertainty of each and every Saturday was again being played out during the 2008 season. Two of the three marquee teams that I spoke of earlier were doing their part to try to regain traction after being upset early in the season.

October is a critical month for positioning your team for a run in November. USC and Florida, both losing on the same weekend in September while ranked number 1 and number 2, respectively, rebounded nicely to go 6–1 through October. The Irish, my focus team of the year, had lost twice to stand at 5–2. I didn't think they'd lose *any* games to this point in the season, which just goes to show that games are won and lost on the football field, not on paper.

October 6—Week 5

1. Oklahoma
2. Alabama
3. LSU
4. Missouri
5. Texas
6. Penn State
7. Texas Tech

---

8. USC
9. Ohio State
10. Auburn
11. South Florida
12. Florida
13. Georgia
14. BYU
15. Kansas
16. Vanderbilt
17. Utah
18. Oklahoma State
19. Wisconsin
20. Michigan State
21. Boise State
22. Wake Forest
23. Virginia Tech
24. North Carolina
25. Northwestern

As always, there were a few teams that were either pleasant surprises or had forgotten to show up for the season. Before I break down USC, Florida, and Notre Dame's October, I've got to address my surprise team.

I don't know whether this admission is good or bad on my part—it either says I'm an idiot for not having a team in my preseason poll or it says that I'm fair and, if I miss something, I'm not afraid to recognize it and move forward. I'd like to think of the latter as being the case, because I didn't have the University of Alabama in my preseason poll!

Here was my thinking about the Tide prior to the '08 season. I was looking for a reason other than that it was Alabama to vote them into the preseason top 25. In 2006, the team ended up at 6–7. They then started out strong in '07 by going 6–2, but couldn't keep the roll going and ended up losing four of the next five to finish at a pedestrian 7–6. I ask you, other than the fact that they're the Tide, what had they done to make me think they should be a preseason top 25?

I don't vote on helmet decals, and I am careful about not putting too much into a team's potential. No doubt they had a great head coach in Nick Saban, but that wasn't enough for me to put 'em in the preseason top 25.

After week one, the Tide dismantled the Clemson Tigers, who at the time were ranked number 9 in the country. If the Tide had lost that game, who knows how their season would have gone? Conversely, a Clemson win might have put them on track to have the kind of year most of us expected. An early season test like these two teams really highlights how important momentum is. The Tide win gave their squad plenty of confidence to build on, while the loss by Clemson was one they couldn't overcome.

My next ballot had the Tide at number 11, but even that doesn't seem high enough in retrospect. So how did I miss out on my preseason expectations so badly with the Tide?

First and foremost, I didn't visit Alabama during my spring tour. There was no particular reason I didn't schedule them for a stop; it's just that I couldn't see everybody.

If I'd seen the Tide, I'd have seen just how physical they were. You can't hide that asset—and if you *don't* have it, you can't hide that, either. Alabama came out playing with an edge of toughness and determination that had been lacking in the program. Sure, the Tide were playing with a lot of young, unproven players, yet I'm convinced—*again*—that Nick Saban recruits players who don't wear skirts. Saban's a man's man. He reminds me a whole lot of Steve Spurrier in his days with the Florida Gators. Spurrier had a reputation for coaching great quarterbacks. After all, Spurrier had won the Heisman as a QB for the Gators in 1966. In fact, he's the only coach to have won the Heisman as a QB and then coached a Heisman-winning QB, in Danny Wuerffel.

But my comparison of Saban to Spurrier is based on their reputations for being really hard on QBs. The expectation he had for his QB was to be near-perfect. Even today, now that he's head coach of the South Carolina Gamecocks, I get a rather tart reply when I ask Steve about his QB. "Oh, Craig . . . I don't know . . . we'll give one of 'em a try, and if he ain't gettin' it done, we'll try somebody else. Sometimes I just get tired of looking at the same guy out there messin' up."

A notable example was displayed back in 1997, in a game against favored Florida State. The Seminoles had a great defense, so Spurrier, in an attempt to make sure his QBs knew what he wanted out of each play, decided to rotate Doug Johnson and Noah Brindise throughout the game. It worked, as the Gators upset FSU 32–29. Around that time in the '90s, when Spurrier was establishing his reputation, I was asked on air by Chris Fowler during a *GameDay* show what I thought of Spurrier's handling of his QBs. My answer was more about how I'd feel as a dad with my kid playing QB for Steve. I said that no doubt the guy's a great QB coach, but no way I'd want my QB son to play for Spurrier. There's already enough pressure and demands on a QB, and the last thing a kid needs is a coach that makes the player feel he has to look over his shoulder. Too many head games for my comfort.

Now, it's widely known in the media world that if you say something negative about Spurrier, you're apt to get the cold shoulder—at a minimum. At the end of that '97 season, Spurrier and my buddy Fowler met up in New York after one of the awards shows, and CF got an earful from Spurrier about how

"Craig James doesn't know his ass from a hole in the ground about QBs!" Compared to him, he's right. I'll admit that. But Steve missed my point on his coaching style. As a former player, I wouldn't have liked playing for a guy who had such a short leash, especially for QBs.

But I also said on the air that *if* you decided to play for Spurrier, you knew what you'd signed up for. My TV partner Jesse Palmer played for him, and I think Jesse respects him and had a great time playing QB for the Gators. Jesse knew going in that he was agreeing to play for a man who was quick to verbally pound his QBs. Knowing Jesse as I do now, I'm not surprised he agreed to play for Spurrier. Jesse isn't your typical QB; the dude's from Canada and is as polite and hospitable as any buddy I've ever had. But I also know that he's a tough son of a gun. He's got the kind of grit that if a fight breaks out and his buddy's in trouble, the Royal Mountie is on the way to help. I'm confident that if I'm ever in a bind, he's there for me. That might surprise many to hear that of the man who once played a star role as *The Bachelor*. Oh, don't get me wrong, Jesse will gladly play the role of a gentleman. Holy mackerel, is he ever popular with the ladies! I crack up when these young teenagers come up for a picture with him. These youngsters don't really know who he is, but their moms do!

It's also funny that I worked not only with Jesse, but for a couple of years I also worked with Doug Flutie. Both guys are popular, but Flutie is off-the-charts popular. Everybody seems to have seen his Hail Mary pass while playing for Boston College. While Palmer gets all the young ladies' attention for pics, Flutie gets all the hairy-nosed men coming up to him.

I've made the comparison of Saban to Spurrier for a reason: both are excellent coaches who win. Both are demanding, too. The Tide's team is well aware of what Saban expects. So I have no sympathy for any player who's got a bellyache because of Saban's coaching demands.

I've never played or coached with Saban, but I'm told that he's consistent in his approach—he's tough, hard, and gets after it, which are exactly the characteristics his team displays on the field. I know this. I look forward to seeing the Tide during spring practices of 2009.

• • •

Out west, Pete Carroll had his Trojans back on track. I'll never forget the image I had of them leaving the field the night of their loss in '08 to Oregon State. They walked off rather methodically; I could sense their disappointment. This was a different walk than that of most teams walking off a field following a defeat. Their collective body language yielded a single vibe from a team that knew it had just placed itself into a tough spot for the rest of the season. Plus, they were physically beat up, and were uncertain about the status of their emotional defensive leader, All-American Ray Mauluga. The Trojans didn't know how badly his knee was injured—a season-ending injury would have been as big a loss as that game was on the field.

Part of the reason USC looked so dejected was because they were a team of great athletes who understood the system. The Trojans have a realistic annual goal of playing for the national championship. Lots of teams talk about it, but most don't have the players or the coaches to get there. Pete Carroll has won national championships as well as Pac-10 titles. So not only does *he* believe in himself and his system, so do his assistant coaches and his players.

We can all relate to this inner confidence, perhaps as a result of something we've done in some personal way. In a crazy way,

I relate to it through my business ventures. I think back to the first time I wandered into the hay business. Growing up around a farming family, I generally knew what to do, but I had never actually pulled off a massive production of hay. I remember seeing those first few thousand bales lying in the field and thinking, Okay, we can do this! You must have s story, too, about how *you* felt after "getting it done."

The same success story has to happen in coaching, too. And Carroll's previous accomplishments gave him the personal conviction to attack this early-season loss. I'm sure Pete was bummed, too, but he didn't have time to lie around and sulk—and he obviously didn't, because his team responded nicely to go 6–1 through the month of October.

How nice? The Trojans went on a tear, demolishing their next four opponents—all Pac-10 foes—by a victory margin of 158–20. This impressive streak was exactly what the Trojans needed to get back in the minds of the national voters. No doubt USC had built a platform for a run during the month of November and a shot at the national championship.

While USC was doing their thing out west, the Gators were on a roll of their own down south. Like Carroll, Urban Meyer's experience and past successes gave him and his players the needed confidence to get back on track after their 1-point loss to Ole Miss. As you could see in my ballot, I had penalized the Gators pretty good for losing at home to unranked Ole Miss. They were sitting at number 12 and had more ground to make up in the polls than did the Trojans. But the benefit of playing in a stronger and more-respected conference would give Florida a more likely chance to move back into a position for the national championship.

I was impressed with the overall execution and matter-of-fact attitude the Gators showed through October. They beat Arkansas and Kentucky and trounced defending national champion LSU.

For me, that was a real statement game as to the power and depth of the Gators. Tim Tebow's pledge to will his team back in the race was evident on the field with his leadership and success.

Meanwhile, up north, the Irish were starting to lose a few media folks who'd jumped on their preseason bandwagon. I was still on board, but after the Irish loss in mid-September to Michigan State and a close loss on the road to North Carolina, things weren't adding up to the kind of season coach Charlie Weis had envisioned. Most teams who'd gone 3–9 the previous season would have been thrilled to start the next year with a 5–2 record. Not the Irish—not a school with such a huge budget for football and with facilities that are second to none.

The thing about the Irish is that the fans either love 'em or hate 'em. In my opinion, the Irish are good for college football. NBC doesn't carry their games just for the heck of it. Fans tune in to watch Notre Dame whether they are winning or not.

But change is in the air; Weis knows it and understands it. He's paid a lot of money to win games and play in BCS bowl games. That air of change is why I was so interested in Notre Dame during the early parts of the 2008 season. Remember, at this point in the season I was still on board with Weis's chances of getting the job done. November was going to be really big for the Irish. They'd have to win a lot of games to keep the boo-birds at bay.

• • •

Throughout this book I've discussed how important the combination of coaching and talent is. For winning teams, these two ingredients are a must. In chapter 5 I listed the key ingredients necessary for a coach to be successful. Now, let's look at the talent. What's the makeup of a great player? Who are some of the greatest players and leaders I've observed playing college football?

Well, the following three players are warriors! There have been loads of really good college football players, yet these three stand out in my mind above and beyond all others.

Tim Tebow

Tim's emotional apology during a postgame press conference following Florida's loss at home to unranked Ole Miss will go down in college football lore. For Gators' fans it *certainly* will. Tim's pledge to the Gator nation to outwork his teammates and to push them to their utmost potential was above and beyond the call of duty. The loss to Ole Miss wasn't all his doing. But Tim's tearful apology motivated not only the players but the coaches, too. One of the things I love about Tim is that he genuinely cares about winning. Yeah, I realize there are lots of other players out there who want badly to win, too. But Tim's the leader of his team both on and off the field. His reputation of being fanatical in the offseason for pushing himself is contagious.

Coach Meyer is filling his locker room with loads of talent, but there are lots of talented teams around the country that never seem to play up to their bloodlines. Why? Some blame has to go to the coaches for not knowing how to motivate their players, but nine times out of ten it's the result of a talented team not having a superstar to lead by example. I think Tim's a *heck* of a college player and an example of how each individual is supposed to act.

In terms of ability, notice that I said "heck" of a player. In my opinion, there have been lots of players over the years who were more talented than Tim. I know I just fired up the Gator nation, but I could make the argument that his teammate Percy Harvin is a better player/athlete than Tebow. Harvin's fast and quick and can run with the ball as well as catch it. Harvin's got Sunday talent. But hear what I'm saying when I recognize Tim as one of the all-time leaders/players of college football. Remember, I'm placing him alongside two other football greats as being above all the rest. Tim's one of the all-time great college football players because of *all* the things he means to his team.

Michael Irvin

This beast of a player led his Hurricane teammates to an undefeated 12–0 season in 1987 and a national championship. While at Miami, Michael became known as "The Playmaker." During his 'Canes days he became the school's all-time receiving leader and was notorious for raising his hands and pointing to the sky after scoring a touchdown. Michael says it was in respect and acknowledgment of his father in heaven.

Like Tebow with his highly recruited Gators teammates, Irvin was surrounded by no telling how many future first-round draft picks. Michael's love for life and people inspired his teammates to work beyond their comfort level. I've known Michael since his early days with the Dallas Cowboys when he was a first-round draft choice in 1988. We became business partners and friends, as I was the cohost of *The Michael Irvin Show*, a weekly half-hour TV show that aired around the state of Texas.

No player I've ever seen comes close to matching Michael's vocal leadership. The Playmaker makes Tim Tebow seem like he's playing with the mute button pushed. Irvin was able to push his teammates so hard because he worked side by side with them, encouraging them and earning their respect with his own determination. Sound familiar? It should: Tebow and Irvin share a similar passion for perfection and for winning on the football field.

Vince Young

Vince Young is the best college football player I've ever seen. I watched him elevate himself and his teammates to victory in back-to-back Rose Bowls. Like Tebow and Irvin, Young was the leader of his Longhorns and was respected by everybody. Tebow was more vocal on the field than Young, and Irvin was much more animated; but Young led by example—with his body and with plays made on the field. His performance inspired those around him to play better than they were normally capable of playing.

Young led his '04 team to an 11–1 record and victory over Michigan in the Rose Bowl. I was on the sidelines for that game and remember visiting with Vince before the game and wishing him luck. Young was Mr. Cool, calm and collected. His presence on the field was special. He was different; his teammates knew it and so did his opponents. It was an air of confidence, not cockiness. Young's performance during the 2005 season was stunning. The 'Horns went 12–0 during the regular season and matched up in the 2006 Rose Bowl against USC.

I think we all agree that great players step up in big games and elevate themselves above everybody else on the field. The stage was set for Young to end his career in storybook fashion. USC was the defending national champion and had a thirty-four-game winning streak. Part of that run was because they had two Heisman Trophy winners on the same team. Quarterback Matt Leinart had won the award in 2004, and the next year's trophy went to his backfield mate, dual threat Reggie Bush. Is that star power or what? And it didn't hurt that the Rose Bowl is a home game for USC. So everything was lined up for USC to win the game; at the same time, it was set up for Vince Young to show who the real hoss was in town.

I've been using the term "warrior" to describe these three remarkable players. Here's an example of why Vince is one.

In the middle of the fourth quarter USC was in control and appeared to be heading for a victory. They had the momentum, and their fans were into the game, too. I was standing on the Texas sidelines; USC had scored and there was a TV timeout. USC's known to get together as a group on their sidelines after a score and before the following kickoff to get even more fired up. They start jumping around in a circle and dancing, all the while getting the attention of the opposing team. Their antics are designed to fire themselves up, but just as importantly to get in the heads of their opponents.

During this TV timeout, I was standing behind Young and his teammates. The 'Horns were waiting for the officials to signal for them to take the field for the kickoff return. Across the field I saw the Trojans dancing around. Young and his teammates were watching USC celebrate. The Texas bench's vibe was terrible; everybody in the stadium could sense a Trojan victory at hand. The Longhorns players were standing behind Vince when all of a sudden he put his helmet on and started gently bouncing around. I could hear him say, "All right! Here we go, fellas! Let's get it on!" It was a defining moment for me and what I think of Vince Young. Young had stood there watching USC having fun, almost mocking the Longhorns and their fans. Young could have easily accepted the reality of the moment and how tough it was going to be for his team to overcome so much adversity.

Throughout the game the two teams had gone back and forth, but here it was in the fourth quarter and the Trojans were leading 38–26 with only 6:42 to play. No problem for VY—Young confidently took the field and took control of the game. The 'Horns went on a 69-yard scoring drive, with Young accounting for *all* the yards, to make the score 38–33 with 2:39 to play. It was still highly unlikely the Longhorns would win this game. After all, they were facing what at the time was billed as one of the all-time best offenses in college football, led by Matt Leinart and Reggie Bush.

But the Longhorns' defense rose to the occasion to stop the Trojans, getting the ball back in the hands of the best player on the field. Vince Young had come in second during that current season's Heisman Trophy race to Bush, who at that point was watching from the other sideline.

Remember what I said about Young's demeanor? Tebow and Irvin were animated and verbal. At this point in the game, Vince didn't have to say a word. His teammates knew they had the best player in the country standing with them. I've been to a lot of great games over the years, but none comes close to the intensity and excitement of this Rose Bowl matchup.

Young took his team down to the Trojans goal line with 19 seconds to play. It was fourth and 5 from the 8-yard line. Keep in mind that Young was doing this against the USC defense, which as always was stocked full of NFL talent. At the snap of the ball everything seemed to go in slow motion—especially the Trojans' defense. Young took the snap and proceeded to weave his way through the Trojans' defense as if he were back in elementary school playing youth football. Young scored the winning touchdown and, for me, history was made. I'd just witnessed the single best performance by a player in a game.

Everybody on the USC defense, everybody in the stands, and everybody at home knew Young was going to run the ball. But this champion elevated himself to Superman status and denied all eleven Trojan defenders. I remember turning to John Saunders and saying, "There, my friend, is the best player in college football!" Saunders agreed, as did most anybody with a fair mind. Even Trojans fans would have a hard time not admitting that.

For the numbers, Young rushed and threw for more than 200 yards, accounting for nearly 500 yards total offense. You might have heard the saying "There was a buzz after the game." Well, this was a stunning buzz, as the nearly hundred thousand fans stood around long after the game ended trying to comprehend what they'd just witnessed.

•　•　•

Now back to 2008, three-quarters of the way through the season. There were a few teams and players emerging that were making things interesting as college football entered its final month of play.

My first surprise team was Penn State. My preseason ballot had the Nittany Lions at number 22, but by the end of October, they were 9–0 and just coming off a nice victory over preseason Big Ten favorite Ohio State. I now had them ranked number 2 in the country. Penn State wasn't a team with a headliner superstar. Rather, it was a team playing well together led by their coach, Joe Paterno. Joe Pa was entering his fifty-ninth season on the staff of PSU, with this season his forty-third as head coach. It was reasonable for anybody to wonder why Joe Pa was still coaching at the age of eighty-two.

Many talk shows were doing their usual second-guessing of Joe Pa's decision to continue coaching. For the record, and as I've stated many times on the air, Joe Pa should be allowed to coach as long as he wants to at Penn State. However, after announcing the previous season's 2007 Alamo Bowl game between Texas A&M and PSU and having spent time around Joe Pa during that week, I had my doubts as to whether he should be coaching in 2008. He just seemed to have aged a lot, and I wondered if he still had the necessary spunk to coach as he had in previous years.

At this point in my own career, I had to tread carefully on TV when talking about Joe. During the 2006 season, while doing the studio show for ABC, I was in New York watching Penn State play Wisconsin. The Badgers were led by first-year head coach Bret Bielema. At the very end of the first half, Bielema took advantage of a new rule that allowed him to run out the clock at the end of the half and therefore keep PSU from getting the ball. The rule for that year was that the clock started when the kicker's foot hit the ball. So Wisconsin kicked the ball out of bounds a couple of times and the half ended. Joe Pa was furious!

Our TV cameras showed Joe Pa engaging the officials in a spirited way as he headed toward the locker room. As we always do, our game sideline reporter interviewed the coach and then sent it right to our studio show in New York. Bottom line: rookie head coach Bielema had outfoxed Joe Pa, and it pissed off Paterno. So here we were live in New York within seconds of the shot of Joe Pa going off, and Saunders laughs and turns to me for a comment. I was laughing, too, and said, "Atta way, Bielema; way to get after that old fart!"

I said it with a smile and meant it as a term of endearment. People say it all the time. As a matter of fact, Joe Pa and former Iowa coach Hayden Fry used to call each other "old farts."

Well, the Penn State faithful didn't take my comment kindly. The ABC/ESPN communications department received a call from the PSU sports information director demanding that I issue an on-air apology to Joe Pa. When confronted by ESPN about the apology, I at first thought they were kidding me. But they weren't. I'd been doing TV for nearly twenty years and had never had to issue an on-air apology. I've got this little edit man in my head who's always served me well. I stay away from things that are dicey. And my edit man didn't stop me from saying what I said about Joe Pa.

So my position with my bosses was that I didn't think I needed to issue an apology. Bottom line: I sat down in our green room in New York and seriously contemplated telling my bosses that I wasn't going to do it. If I didn't, chances were that I wouldn't have been allowed back on the air that day, and my world would have been jammed up with turmoil as a result.

ESPN understood both parties' positions. I decided to overcome my ego and pride and issue an apology. It was a ten-second explanation that I meant no disrespect to Joe Pa, and that was it. I still get pissed just thinking about it. ESPN should have stood by me and told Penn State that I had been a huge supporter of Joe Pa over the years and an apology wasn't warranted. ESPN communications was all concerned that this was going to become a huge national deal. It never materialized into anything but a local-paper story at PSU. Sure, it fired up the die-hard Joe Pa fans, and I still hear from them. But there's nothing unique about that concept. I hear from almost all schools around the country about things I say regarding their team or coach or players.

I did call Joe Pa the next week to make sure he knew I wasn't being disrespectful. Guess what? He could not have cared less about what I said. He was far more upset about his team losing to Wisconsin 13–3 than he was about what I might have said in New York. I moved on from the supposed controversy, and so did he. (For the record, you'll later see that I voted Joe Pa Coach of the Year with my AP ballot after the 2008 season. I greatly respect Joe Pa and what he has done for college football.)

Surprise team number two was the Texas Longhorns. My preseason expectation for them was a little better than that of PSU's—I had them ranked in the preseason at number 17. The Longhorns were much better than I thought they'd be based on what I'd seen on my spring tour. Colt McCoy was having a great season and had become a complete player. Colt had spent a lot of time studying and preparing to be successful during the offseason. I didn't doubt he'd play well, but I didn't think he'd have go-to receivers who would allow him to shine as he'd done through October. Not only did Colt mesh with his receivers Jordan Shipley and Quan Cosby, he'd also improved his speed to become a much better runner than he'd been. If he hadn't actually gotten faster, he was sure playing as if he had.

Mack Brown was doing a great job coaching his team and keeping them focused on their task one game at a time. The Longhorns had beaten OU, Missouri, and Oklahoma State in a three-game run with each of those teams either in the top 10 or ranked there at one point during the season. Mack's a genius at getting his team emotionally prepared to play. After the OU win in the Red River Rivalry, Mack had his team perform a ceremonial burial back in Austin of the OU game ball. He was trying to make sure his team had gotten over that win and were ready to play their next opponent. I liked his idea a lot, and it worked.

My other surprise team through October was the Red Raiders of Texas Tech.

Tech was blazing through their opponents in typical Mike Leach style, scoring lots of points along the way. I was wearing two hats when following the Red Raiders. First and foremost was my "Dad hat," pulling for my son Adam. As an analyst, the Red Raiders were right where I thought they'd be—undefeated at 8–0 and playing November 1 against top-ranked Texas, with a shot at playing for the conference title. My preseason ballot for Tech had them at number 12, and by the end of October they'd moved up to number 7. Back in the spring I kept telling Adam and his teammates that the only thing separating them from the other top-10 programs was a mind-set that they were going to win. Not just win, but win it all.

Based on what I'd seen of Tech, they had the bodies and the athletes to win it all. And strategically, Tech was executing on both offense and defense. But would they have it mentally?

Would Leach be able to pull the right emotional strings to win week in and week out like OU, USC, Texas, and other consistent big-time programs?

Two things were different about this Tech team. First, they could run the ball, and that balance was driving defenses nuts. Second, Tech was playing much better defense. They were bigger inside with their defensive tackles and linebackers, and they were making stops when they had to. We'll cover their game with Texas in chapter 10, because it turned out to be thrilling, to say the least.

Not all my surprises were good. My preseason ballot had Auburn at number 11, and, remember, I didn't even have Alabama on it. I must have had bad coffee that trip and thought I was seeing Auburn when in fact it was the Tide! I wish that were the excuse. No kidding, at Auburn I saw a bunch of really good-looking players. I told their coach, Tommy Tuberville, that he should be commended for the work he'd done to assemble such a talented roster.

But the team I saw practicing in the spring didn't show up for the '08 season. By the end of October, they were 4–4, including a loss at Vanderbilt. The boo-birds were out in force, and Tuberville was on the hot seat.

Tommy's a heck of a coach and a good guy, but he was lacking a warrior. Heck, the player didn't even have to be of that stature—Tommy needed just one star player who could motivate and inspire the rest of the team to play with confidence and attitude.

Auburn's woes weren't just about the players—the coaching staff deserved their share of the blame, too. Auburn had two new coordinators to break in. I'm always concerned when a team is learning from a new coordinator, but for some reason, I cut Auburn slack when it came to break-in time. Tony Franklin was running the offense, and Paul Rhoads the defense. Both are excellent coaches with solid résumés.

The real downfall was Auburn's inability to score points. The defense was okay, but they couldn't carry the load of the entire team while the offense continued to learn a new system. Franklin's one of the gurus of the run and shoot, or the West Coast, or any other name you want to put on an offense that spreads you out and throws the ball. The key to that offensive scheme is the quarterback. The QB doesn't have to be a Heisman candidate, but he needs to have knowledge of the offense and a strong enough arm to make the throws. Auburn had a young man in Chris Todd who'd transferred from Texas Tech and had good credentials. He knew the offense, and it was widely hoped he'd be their guy. But Todd had a previous injury to his throwing arm that never fully recovered.

Don't get me wrong. There's a lot more to blame for Auburn's collapse than a sore/weak arm of a transfer QB! It is another glaring example of how important team chemistry is—not just with the players but the coaching staff, too. Texas was winning because of their overall chemistry. Ironically, UT was breaking in a new defensive coordinator in Will Muschamp, who'd just left Auburn to join Mack Brown in Austin. The Longhorns were on a midseason roll and ranked number 1 in the country in large part due to the success of their defense. So while a coaching change is a challenge for any team, it can't be an automatic excuse.

October 27

1. Texas: Great 3-week run
2. Penn State: From #22 to #2
3. Alabama: Off charts to #3
4. OU: Despite loss, a very talented team
5. Florida: Focused!
6. Oklahoma State: What an offense

7. Texas Tech: Could be for real w/defense playing better
8. USC: Like Florida—focused after loss
9. Ohio State: Hangin' on
10. LSU: Reeling w/no QB
11. Georgia
12. Utah: Cinderella?
13. TCU: Hard playing—as usual
14. Georgia Tech: How 'bout 1st-year coach Paul Johnson
15. Pitt: Young & talented
16. Missouri: Oh, boy—slipping
17. Kansas
18. Boise State
19. Northwestern: Nice start
20. Tulsa: We'll see how good they are 1st weekend Nov vs Arkansas
21. Boston College: Can't figure 'em out
22. BYU: Hard core & good
23. Minnesota
24. FSU: Big win to end Oct vs Virginia Tech
25. Arizona: Love Mike Stoops & staff

• • •

The conclusion of the '08 season was going to be awesome! The run for a shot at the national championship had several realistic possibilities. Coaches were about to start their lobbying to the voters as to why their team should be considered. OU was my number-1 team, but they had lost in the middle of October to number-5 Texas. However, Coach Bob Stoops didn't let his team go in the tank and quit. As you can see on my ballot, they were still ranked number 4, even after that loss. And Stoops was telling his guys to hang in there because the Longhorns still had to face number-7 Texas Tech in Lubbock.

The upcoming month of November was also the time we'd be able to watch and appreciate some big rivalries: Notre Dame–USC, Michigan–Ohio State, Alabama–Auburn, USC–UCLA, and Texas–Texas A&M. And even though OU against Oklahoma State isn't typically considered a national rivalry, these two teams were going to wrap up the regular season with a chance for OU to win the Big 12 title and get a shot at the national championship—so all eyes were going to be on that game.

With a lot of big bowl games on the line and a shot at the national championship totally open to several schools, the conclusion of 2008 was great for some and big-time disappointing for others.

THE GREATEST RIVALRIES

I was sitting in church many years ago when my pastor, Jack Graham, started talking about how we Americans have gotten away from celebrating traditions. It's as if we've gotten too busy in our daily grinds to stop and enjoy life the way previous generations did. Sure, we still enjoy Thanksgiving, Christmas, Valentine's Day, and the Fourth of July, but a lot of traditions have gone away.

I can remember going to church as a little boy on Sunday mornings and then hanging out all afternoon at our house with friends and family stopping by to eat and play. I loved it—we got to eat a ton and then had plenty of cousins and friends to play football with out in the yard.

Tradition can mean a lot of different things to a lot of people. It can be as simple as sitting down at the dinner table each night to eat with your family (tell me *that* one hasn't faded away!). For my brother and me, as little boys we were lucky that our grandfathers took the time to have a routine with us.

Chris and I had a tradition with my Papa Boyd. Every morning he'd take us into town in his old 1950s pickup truck to Melvin Williams's grocery store. It must have been ten miles to the store, and every time we'd go over a hill, Papa would put the truck in neutral so we'd coast to the bottom. I think the game was to see how far we could go without putting it back in gear. As I get older, I appreciate being blessed with vivid memories like this one. Papa would buy us each a Dr Pepper and a Fudgsicle every time. You can imagine us driving back to the house sitting next to Papa in the cab—there wasn't a backseat, and there *certainly* wasn't any air conditioning—and by the time we'd gone a mile or two, Chris and I would have chocolate running down our faces and all over our shirts.

My other grandfather, Papa James, was a county commissioner. The tradition or routine I had with him was riding the country roads checking in on his work crews. I used to love riding on the big, heavy equipment, pretending I was driving. Chris and I thought we were big-time important. The best part of driving the roads and working with Papa James was lunch. The county barn was the headquarters for all of the workers and a gathering spot to shoot the bull. This barn had an ice maker, which in the 1960s was a big deal. And the ice it produced was the kind of shaved ice you get with a snow cone. Chris and I ate that ice like it was a double-meat cheeseburger.

The simple traditions or routines that many of us have stored in the backs of our minds are often forgotten. As Pastor Graham said, our lives have become so busy that we've forgotten to stop and enjoy the little things in life.

Fortunately in college football, we haven't forgotten our past or the celebrations of the time-tested rivalry games. I strongly believe that we are so committed to these rivalries in part because they are one of the few things remaining that we take time to enjoy.

November and December provide a strong dose of traditions for college football fans. I still get fired up in early November on that first cold night when the air is filled with the season's first smell of the smoke from fireplaces. The night chill, the fireplace smell, and the background sound of the local high school band practicing are enough to make me want to bend over and touch my toes!

So here we were in 2008, with yet another perfect setup for an end-of-the-year run to rival any of the great ones. I'd started the year thinking that USC and Ohio State were the two best teams in the country. The wild rush to the end started in November with USC ranked at number 9 and Ohio State at number 10—both on the outside looking in and needing a lot of things to happen before they would get back in the conversation of national title contenders.

The backstretch of the season wasn't looking too good for Notre Dame. Entering November with a 5–2 record, the Irish had no room for error. Keep in mind that this was a team that not only I thought had a chance to be unbeaten at this time, but so did their head coach, Charlie Weis. Maybe it was warmer than usual in South Bend, and their citizens/fans hadn't cranked up the fireplaces, yet. The smell of autumn hadn't invaded the senses of the Irish team as they lost three of the first four games in this telling month. But they did have a season finale with long-time rival USC, and if they could muster a monster of a game and somehow upset the Trojans, then some of the disappointment of '08 could be erased.

•　•　•

Let's kick off the rivalry tour with one close to my backyard—the Red River Rivalry: The University of Texas versus Oklahoma Sooners. Growing up as a kid in Texas, it was hard not to know about this game. Living in Houston, I was surrounded by UT fans. It seemed like they all drove either pickup trucks (the younger folks) or Cadillacs with big hood ornaments (the older, more established folks)! Regardless of age, though, they all seemed to wear cowboy boots. The style back then was a high-heeled boot with a pointed toe—so pointed that you could smash a three-inch cockroach in the corner of a room with no problem.

In Houston, where the humidity is abundant, it seemed like cockroaches lived in colonies of twelve, so a good pair of "roach killers" was a must. You had to have that point to get into the corner. I bet you could line up a room full of barefoot men standing against a wall and tell which ones came from Texas in the '70s. Without even knowing their ages, you'd recognize them because I'm sure their toes are bunched-up crooked from squeezing into those pointed boots.

What do boots and car styles have to do with OU–Texas? Lots, because it's the personality of the fans that makes these games special. Year in and year out, these same fans are at the game acting and playing their part to continue the traditions so special to the event. The names of players change, but not the makeup of the fans.

The first game played between these two schools was in 1900, when Oklahoma was still called Oklahoma Territory! Texas's team was referred to as Varsity, while OU was simply known as the Oklahoma team. Since 1912, the games have been played in Dallas, and beginning in 1932, they've all been battled on the field at the Cotton Bowl.

The Cotton Bowl sits in what is called Fair Park, the site of the annual State Fair of Texas, which provides the perfect atmosphere for pregame and postgame activities. While 92,000 fans attend the game, those unable to get a ticket aren't left out of the partying scene. They hang around the State Fair, helping to create an atmosphere that is fun and special.

The 2008 game had plenty of buildup, and rightly so. OU entered the game ranked number 1 in the country, while UT entered at number 5. It appeared going in that the winner would have the inside track to playing for the national championship. Plus, this game featured two top Heisman contenders: OU QB Sam Bradford and UT QB Colt McCoy.

Earlier I talked about the importance of having a warrior on your team, and how that individual can elevate his teammates to perform to their utmost abilities. Bradford and McCoy meet those requirements! Bradford's more outwardly subdued—he's intense, but not real animated with his body. He lets his arm talk for him. McCoy's much more demonstrative—and whereas Bradford gets it done by throwing the ball, McCoy gets it done with his legs, too.

It was a beautiful sunny day in Dallas. OU jumped out fast on Texas and had a nice lead. It was almost as if UT was initially surprised or overwhelmed by OU's size and speed. And I think OU might have let up just a smidgen, thinking they were going to blow out the Longhorns. That mind-set is usually a death knell for a team, which is exactly how it turned out for OU.

McCoy and his teammates simply outplayed OU in the second half. Their victory wasn't about strategy as much as it was about momentum and execution. Texas's victory would vault them to the number-1 ranking in the country. So now they'd have to play with the bull's-eye painted on their chests.

Would the Longhorns have the strength and focus to handle their next three-week run—with an unexpected showdown from a conference foe?

• • •

During the summer months, college football fans are notorious for schedule browsing. How many times have we looked up our teams of interest and done the run-through, trying to determine who our team will beat and who they'll lose to? Even the preseason publications try to predict certain wins and losses for each team, as well as swing games. Jesse Palmer always jacks with Chris Fowler about how during our meetings with players and coaches

CF always seems to ask, "Is this is a swing game?" Basically, Chris is asking whether the game will make, break, or otherwise alter a team's season.

Of all the games to ponder prior to the 2008 season, I guarantee you that not one fan in America predicted that the game of the year would be between Texas and Texas Tech. Sure, we all knew that it had the makings of being a really important game—important, perhaps, for the national picture, but of paramount importance for the Big 12 title.

UT was riding a monster wave of momentum after beating top-ranked OU in Dallas. The 'Horns followed up that victory with straight wins against two more top-10 teams, Missouri and Oklahoma State. Could Texas make it four wins in a row over top-10 teams?

Mack Brown's reputation for finding ways to get his teams mentally and physically ready to play would be put to the test. Leading up to the Tech game, Mack brought in a bunch of Navy SEALs to talk to the Longhorns about how to stay focused and on track in order to handle adversity. Obviously, the challenge for the UT team was trying to muster up enough energy to "do it one more time!"

At this point, Tech was ranked number 5, and UT was number 1. I can tell you that it's hard to play back-to-back *big* games, let alone four in a row. The second week of big games is easy compared to the third and forth weeks, because you're more or less still on a high from the previous game. I don't care how many mind games you play, a player's body and mind just can't handle four weeks in a row of intensity.

And in this particular matchup, the Longhorns' defense was going to be doubly challenged because Tech liked to spread their offense from sideline to sideline. So UT was going to have to cover a lot of ground on each and every play. Unlike a game against a run offense where the football stays in the middle of the field the whole game, UT was going to be taxed physically and mentally from the opening snap to the final whistle—and this one came all the way down to that final whistle.

I don't want to paint the picture that Texas would have won if they had been fresh entering this contest—far from it. Tech had a really good team, and they were much better in '08 because they didn't just throw the football, they ran it, too. That means so much in a game—to have the ability to run *and* throw. I've always said that when you pass protect, it's like taking your gal to a dance, whereas when you run the ball, it's like going to a street fight. The attitude of a running team is one of power and dominance, while the passing game is all about finesse.

Now, Tech wasn't a team that wanted to run it forty times a game, but their ability to successfully run it twenty-plus times was a significant difference for this particular team because their air game was rock solid.

The game started, and Tech jumped all over Texas! The Red Raiders' fans were given a national TV audience to show off their team spirit, and they didn't disappoint. Tech led at halftime, 22–6. I was sitting in New York doing the studio show for this game and was going nuts, to say the least. Brent Musberger was calling the game, and when my son Adam caught a pass in the third quarter, Musberger said, "I imagine Adam's dad is in New York pretty excited about now." No doubt, Brent—off-air I could root and holler for my son all I wanted to! As a matter of fact, Mack Brown would be disappointed in me if I didn't pull for my son. Mack is the perfect gentleman and always asks about my boys.

Coming out after halftime, Texas got a desperately needed break when Jordan Shipley returned a punt in the middle of the third quarter for a touchdown. UT actually got a double break on the play because a flag was thrown by an official and yet was picked up after the play ended. The official said that a clipping that was called on the return against UT hadn't really happened. The officials waved off the call. Baloney! TV replays showed it was clearly an illegal block in the back and therefore should have negated the UT touchdown.

Shipley's return pumped oxygen into his teammates, and Tech was going to have to fight to hold off the number-1 team in the country. The Longhorns had pride and character, and their leader Colt McCoy was ready to pull off the comeback. The score at this point was Tech 22, UT 13.

They would hold the lead until late in the fourth quarter, when McCoy took UT 80 yards for a touchdown and their first lead of the game at 33–32 with just 1:28 to go.

It's funny how fans are. Throughout this entire contest I'd been getting jammed with text messages on my cell phone from Tech fans hootin' and hollerin' about the Red Raiders. After Texas scored with 1:28 to go and took the lead, I got just one message, which said, "Oh shit!"

That's exactly what everybody was thinking, me included.

Fortunately for Tech, their QB Graham Harrell and All-American receiver Michael Crabtree weren't thinking negatively.

Now Tech needed a break just like the one the Longhorns had gotten in the third quarter with Shipley's punt return TD. Tech moved down the field, looking like they were going to get into field-goal range at a minimum for a chance to win the game. The break came on a Harrell pass that was deflected in the air and landed right in the arms of a UT defender. It looked like the easiest interception ever, but the ball slipped ever so gingerly through the defender's arms, and the game-ending interception was avoided.

So it would come down to perhaps the last play of the game. Tech was on its own 28-yard line with 8 seconds remaining on the clock. It would be a 45-yard field goal from that spot, and Tech had a walk-on, very inexperienced kicker. So Coach Mike Leach decided to run one more play to get a little bit closer for the field-goal attempt.

This was a big-time gamble by Leach because the clock could have very well run out of time and the game would have been over.

Harrell dropped back to pass and heaved the ball toward the right sidelines and his go-to receiver, Crabtree. "Tree" caught the ball around the 10-yard line, and rather than jumping out of bounds to stop the clock, he shed a tackler and darted into the end zone for the game-winning touchdown.

I still get goose bumps recalling that play. Regardless of who you were pulling for, one of the best game-ending plays had just happened. My Thursday partner Chris Fowler was standing on the sidelines right next to the play as it unfolded. A photo of the catch shows Chris in the background, wide-eyed and shouting, "Ahhhh!" It's classic. Chris has seen a ton of great games, yet here he was on his first visit to Lubbock, Texas, watching this remarkable ending. This finish of the year pulled an unbelievable rating of 7.5—meaning that roughly 8.6 million households had watched the game. It was the fifth-most-watched regular-season game ever on ABC.

The Longhorns' effort was valiant, but this night was for the Red Raiders. The Tech victory was setting up a pretty interesting scenario in the Big 12. Texas had beaten OU, and now Tech had beaten UT. In a few weeks, Tech was going to have to play at OU, and the Sooners were nearly perfect in Norman under Bob Stoops. An OU victory in that game would set up a complicated three-way tie in the Big 12.

This 2008 season was a banner year for the Big 12, which put up a strong challenge as the best conference in America against the year-in and year-out best, the SEC. That didn't mean the SEC wasn't strong at the top—Florida, Alabama, and Georgia were darn good teams.

• • •

The next stop on the rivalry tour was to the World's Largest Outdoor Cocktail Party: Florida versus Georgia. The title has been simplified to the Florida-Georgia game (or the Georgia-Florida game on alternate years) in order to get away from a name that might seem to encourage students to drink a bunch that weekend. I'm glad they changed it because there have been way too many alcohol-related incidents reported.

I'd heard for years how this was a great game to see. Man, is it ever an atmosphere! My first experience was back in the '90s. I remember the stuff surrounding the game far more than I do the game itself. The partying at my hotel was crazy. It was still called the World's Largest Outdoor Cocktail Party, and I think the room next to mine was headquarters for the fans. I had fans banging on my door all night before the game. "Hey, James, go Gators!" "Hey, James, you're an idiot!" "Hey, James, better pick the Bulldogs!" The banging and chanting went on all night.

Sometimes rivalries need a little freshening up. Georgia still owns the overall number of wins in this series. They dominated the 1970s and 1980s, but now UF has done the same during the 1990s and 2000s. The game got a little spice in 2007 when Georgia head coach Mark Richt told his team before the game that he wanted them to really celebrate after their team's first touchdown. When UGA scored, the entire bench stormed the field to celebrate. What has become known as the Gator Stomp wasn't appreciated at all by the Gator Nation. They were fired up mad. But for the 2007 game, there wasn't a thing they could do about it as the Bulldogs won the game, 42–30. Florida coach Urban Meyer took the high road for the entire next season and laid low without really responding to the Gator Stomp. Even leading up to the 2008 game, he said revenge wasn't a motivating factor for his team.

On my ballot just before the '08 game I had Florida at number 7 and Georgia at number 8. This was no doubt a huge game, with the winner having the inside track to winning the SEC East and getting back into the mix for a shot at the national title. Whether revenge for the '07 embarrassment was a factor or not, the Gators took advantage of multiple Georgia mistakes and routed the Bulldogs, 49–10. After the game, Coach Meyer admitted that he and his team had not liked the '07 loss very much and definitely wanted to redeem themselves. The Gators got payback, and the win kept them in contention for a shot at the SEC championship and perhaps the national title.

This win by the Gators on a national TV stage also put reigning Heisman winner Tim Tebow squarely back in the race. Tebow was playing extremely well and continued the commitment he made to Gator fans after that loss to Ole Miss to not let his team lose again.

It's at about this point in each season that my role in the studio gets more interesting. Team rankings become really important to schools in the running for a BCS berth. With millions of dollars on the line and the positive exposure that comes with a BCS game, it's easy to understand why coaches are dialed in to what's being said about their teams.

People ask me all the time what the difference is between my job as a game announcer in the booth and my job as an analyst in the studio. Studio work is like looking at a really wide river—one that's a long way across but shallow. I have to be able to comment on Cal or Oregon with the same confidence and level of information that I have for Michigan or Iowa or FSU or North Carolina State. I've got to know what all the major players are up to.

Conversely, announcing a game is like looking at a narrow river that's very deep. I've got to know both teams as if I played for them. Local fans for each squad will know if I say something that is half-baked or off-base. Hard-core fans can hear in your analysis if you're dialed in to their team or not.

I remember listening to the Texas–Texas Tech game earlier in the season and hearing what Kirk Herbstreit was saying about the Red Raiders. Since my son Adam plays for Tech, I had the huge advantage of knowing the real poop on the Red Raiders. Herby was dialed in big-time! I called him after the game and told him he did a great job of being prepared for that game. I was a "local fan" in this instance and would have noticed if he hadn't done his homework. I never want to leave a game with fans thinking I mailed it in and wasn't ready to service that game.

An example of a coach being dialed in to what's being said about his team involves OU coach Bob Stoops. Stoops's defenses are known for being dominant. But during this November run his defense was giving up nearly 30 points a game. On paper that doesn't look too impressive. So I called Bob to ask him about his defense. I'd seen them on tape and had my own thoughts, but I wanted to hear from the man himself. Bob said he didn't have the least bit of concern for his defense—that his unit was playing well each game except for a play here or there. Plus, he said a big reason the Sooners were giving up a lot of points was because his offense was scoring a lot of points on short drives. Therefore, the Sooners' opponents were having a lot more snaps per game and more opportunities to score.

So as an evaluator of a team's overall strength, it's important to look inside the numbers to be able to properly or fairly judge a team. At this point in the season, no coach wants to have his defense questioned by pollsters. Bob took the time with me, knowing that I have a big platform Thursday nights and Saturdays in New York. Bob wanted me to be able to accurately deliver his position and feelings about his team, as well as for me to be better informed when assessing his team's standing with my AP ballot.

Bottom line: credible first-person information is critical to announcing. Very few sportscasters or writers covering college football have first-person information. Yet they use their personal media (radio, TV, or print) to comment on a team or game. Half-cocked at best is how I'd analyze most folks' coverage of college football. I'm sorry to those I've just offended—sometimes the truth hurts. You know the old saying: If the shoe fits . . . Otherwise, to those working hard at getting it right, keep on keepin' on. Great job!

• • •

Staying with OU, the Sooners were set to take on the new hottie of college football: Texas Tech. The Red Raiders were the flavor of choice after beating number-1 Texas and following that win up the next week with a dominant victory over number-7 Oklahoma State, 56–20. The Red Raiders were number 1 on a lot of ballots—mine included. In my opinion, when you beat the best, you go to the top of the class.

So here were the Sooners ranked number 4, with their defense giving up a lot of points and being questioned. The Red Raiders were coming in flying sky-high with their offense and with their defense playing well, too. It was now Tech's turn to see if they could get up for a third-week-in-a-row big-time challenge.

But this challenge was even more difficult given the fact that they were playing at OU—and under Stoops in Norman, the Sooners were sporting a 59–3 record!

Early in the week, Stoops kind of called out his fans and asked them to not just show up, but to come ready to intimidate the visitors. Coaches call on their fans to help them all the time. But the fact that OU was playing to get back into the mix of the Big 12 conversation really excited their fans. They showed up, all right! Tech players told me that they'd never been around anything like the atmosphere they now found themselves in. The OU crowd, combined with their excellent team, were far too much for the Red Raiders.

This wasn't a contest at any point in the game. OU was bigger and faster, period. And that OU defense that had been getting questioned all over the country? They kicked butt and dominated the game. Stoops was right, after all, about his defense. He hadn't been just blowing smoke with me.

•   •   •

OU's win now created a pretty big dilemma for the Big 12, with a three-way tie at the top between OU, Texas, and Texas Tech.

The teams vying for a BCS bowl berth were becoming much clearer. The Big 12 had the three-way tie; the SEC had Florida and Alabama playing in their championship game; and out west, the USC Trojans continued to play dominant football, yet were ranked only around 7 in the country. This lack of respect in the polls certainly didn't sit well with their coach, Pete Carroll. The local media in Los Angeles reported that Carroll came out in defense of a playoff system. Of course, that would make headline news coming from Carroll, so I decided to call Pete for a first-person account.

Pete was open and said he didn't like the way the current system worked, especially because nobody knows *how* it works. Pete said that even he didn't understand the computers' input and output, and he wanted me to stress that this wasn't the first time he'd spoken out against the current system.

In '08, his Trojans apparently were going to have a hard time getting any respect from the voters—not enough to get them back to a shot at the title. I was one of those voters Pete could have been mad at. I had 'em at number 6, but remember, I announced the game earlier in the year when they were upset by unranked Oregon State. I was having a hard time getting beyond that and was looking for some marquee wins to propel them back into the top four. No question USC was playing well, but as always during the season, you have to consider their entire body of work. OU, Texas, Alabama, Florida, and Texas Tech had each played a much tougher schedule to date.

• • •

Speaking of strength of schedule, Texas and their coach, Mack Brown, were lobbying voters as to why his team should play for the national title—appropriate timing for a good ol' rivalry game: Texas A&M at Texas on Thanksgiving night. I grew up closely following this longstanding rivalry and was thrilled to be calling it again.

It was appropriate timing for the game because A&M needed it for a shot at upsetting UT and ruining the Longhorns' season. It was poor timing for UT because they were playing on national TV with all of the nation's voters watching. UT was supposed to whip up on the Aggies. And for those of you who have played in a rivalry game, you know that just winning it is a big deal. But Texas was heavily favored, and so the voters were going to expect nothing less than a whippin' on the Aggies.

Plus, this game was a late-season showcase for UT QB Colt McCoy's Heisman run. McCoy was again playing great, and I asked him if he felt the pressure of playing for the Heisman. Colt tried to say he didn't feel it, but he eventually opened up and said that he knew how important it was for his teammates that he win it. No doubt Colt didn't want to let down his teammates.

As for the voters and rankings, Coach Brown was walking a tightrope with how he handled the politicking. Mack had to lobby and sell how good his team was, but if he came across as whining, he'd lose respect *and* votes.

As I'd said about my spring visit to A&M, this team was not on the talent level of the top-25 programs. They weren't even close, and I thought the Longhorns would blow 'em out. The Aggies played a very spirited game and kept the score fairly close for a while before losing, 49–9. This was a weird game to call because the whole time we were announcing we had in our minds that UT had to blow 'em out to stay ranked ahead of OU. That was going to be a challenge because OU had a much stronger opponent two days later against rival Oklahoma State.

My partners and I summed it up by saying that we felt that UT dominated A&M and that being able to dominate a rivalry game is something to appreciate. We also said that Colt McCoy did himself a lot of good by having a spectacular game and keeping his name strongly in the Heisman race.

• • •

Two days later, OU and Oklahoma State squared off, and OU knew what they had to do to pass Texas—win big and impressively. This was a strange scenario. Remember that earlier in the year UT beat OU, Texas Tech beat Texas, and then OU pounded Texas Tech. Now, many fans and experts believed that if OU beat number-12 Oklahoma State, they'd jump Texas in the standings. That would be a critical jump because in a three-way tie the higher-ranked conference team from the Big 12 would go on to play in the Big 12 conference title game.

OU did indeed smack rival OSU, 61–41. And they did indeed jump UT in the rankings. UT fans were furious that a team they'd beaten was going to play in the conference title game, not them. But see, OU had rolled on national TV on back-to-back weeks against great competition and was therefore the current flavor of the month with the voters.

My personal vote and opinion was that UT won on the field head-to-head versus OU, and I couldn't overlook that *fact*. Of course, I was loved by UT fans and hated by OU fans. I suppose even Stoops was pissed at me for taking that stand. I've tried to call him several times, but he hasn't called back. Stoops has to get over that because the day I start playing favorites or saying/voting things I don't really believe is the day I lose credibility. Also, Sooners fans know that 90 percent of the time I'm saying great things about their team. Stoops and other coaches need to remember that I'm paid by ESPN/ABC to do a job and to do it honestly. That's what I try to do week in and week out.

• • •

Here we were at the end of the '08 season. So where were the Irish, and how were they doing? In a word: terribly! Notre Dame had just lost on the road to a Syracuse team that hadn't won a handful of games over the last several years, putting ND at 6–5.

As I stated earlier about rivalries, there've been many teams over the years that have had bad seasons leading up to their rivalry games but then go out and upset their rivals, getting some relief from the previous blunders of the season.

The first Notre Dame–USC game was played in 1926 and is considered one of college football's greatest rivalries. After all, each school has won eleven national championships and produced seven Heisman winners. Not only that, together the two schools have produced more All-Americans than any other schools out there. So as a fan watching this contest, I've always known that the best were playing the best. USC's maintained that standard, while ND has surely dropped from prominence in the eyes of the country.

My first USC-ND game was played in South Bend. It was 1995, and we'd done a *College GameDay* show from the site. I was fired up to finally see this rivalry game in person. John Robinson was USC's coach; Lou Holtz was with ND.

USC came into the game on a roll, ranked number 5, while the Irish were just an okay team, ranked number 17.

It was a beautiful day—perfect weather for football. Lee Corso and I were standing outside the two teams' locker rooms before they came out for warm-ups. We were watching the Irish band walk by on their way to the field. We looked at each other and said how we couldn't believe the size of some of the band members. These big tuba-totin' players had on green skirts, but I wasn't going to crack on 'em—I was impressed.

As soon as the band had left the tunnel and was on the field, out came the USC football team. Coach Robinson came by to say hello, and we wished him luck. But based on what I was looking at standing behind him, Coach wasn't going to need any luck on this day. The USC players looked big and athletic, as good as any team I'd seen.

Next out of the locker room was the Irish squad. When they'd all made it out, Lee and I were both shrugging our shoulders in amazement. Not because the Irish looked good, because they didn't. As a matter of fact, the band looked more imposing than the football team did. Lee and I both concluded that the Irish were going down big-time in this game.

There's something magical about a game at Notre Dame. The stadium's simple, a reminder of the old days and ways. I love history, and while standing on the sidelines of an Irish game, there's an eerie presence about the place. I can't remember who coined the phrase "Wake up the ghosts of the past," but that's the feel of the place for me.

The Irish were in control of this game almost from the opening kick. I remember early on that USC's All-American receiver Keyshawn Johnson was standing in the huddle during a TV timeout looking to the sidelines and telling his teammates that everything was going to be all right. Keyshawn was representative of his other huddle mates—big, talented, and confident (cocky, if you don't like USC!).

But the Irish team wasn't impressed or intimidated by the big, bad Trojans. The smaller, slower Irish defenders were all over Keyshawn and his offense. It looked like a bunch of little gnats running around the field harassing the Trojans.

Notre Dame whipped 'em, 38–10! Sweet Lou had pulled off another improbable victory. During our postgame coverage, we went to long-time college fan/expert Beano Cook for analysis. This was 1995, and for Beano to get to an answer on the current game, you'd have to listen to him start back in 1945 and work his way through the eras to get to his answer. I loved the history lessons, but I remember Beano saying, "Don't ever pick against the Irish at home, young man!"

Maybe it was the ghosts of the past, or the four-leaf clover, or the leprechaun running around, or Touchdown Jesus and the Golden Dome in the background; whatever it was, it was there. The far-outmanned Irish proved again that the game is played on the field—and that in a rivalry game, it's smart to not look at an opponent's record because emotion and the passion to win are part of each player's every thought for the entire sixty minutes of action.

So, would 2008's game between USC and ND be like it was in 1995? It had a similar pregame look and feel. The Irish band still looked big. The Trojans had the physical look of Spartan warriors, and they were playing great football, too. The one big difference was this game was played at USC.

Irish coach Charlie Weis needed his team to at least be competitive. That's not what the Irish fans were thinking, but being realistic, a competitive game by ND could be used as a building block for the future. Better than that, of course, would be for another major rivalry-game upset like their '95 fraternal teammates had done.

Not a chance at all of that happening. USC was powerful and on a roll. The Trojans dominated from the beginning, winning the contest, 38–3. The Irish would end the regular season with a disappointing 6–6 record.

What happened to them? Why didn't they win the nine or ten games I thought they'd win? At the end of the day I just think that the Irish were not in sync in many ways. For sure, the players were trying and wanting to win. It doesn't take long to forget how to win. Here's an Irish team without a superstar (like a Tebow) within the ranks; one who can pick them up and encourage them to go above and beyond. Many teams want to win, but you've got to want to win *bad*! A team has to not want to lose . . . to fear losing . . . to drive themselves in spring workouts to another level of focus and study.

I also don't think Charlie Weis has his staff and their roles coordinated yet, either. That doesn't mean he doesn't have talented assistants. He does, but chemistry and being on the same page aren't things you can just hire and assign. It takes years for a coach to get the right mix of characters on a staff. Charlie will get it figured out; he's done it before and I have no reason to think he won't in South Bend, and soon.

• • •

Here are a few other rivalry games that stand out for me.

Army-Navy

One of the highlights of my broadcasting career came back in 2002 when I was able to announce the Army-Navy game, which was played that year in the New Jersey Meadowlands at Giants Stadium. Navy won big, but for me and many college fans, who wins this game isn't important. What matters most is the tradition of the game and what it stands for.

Army-Navy still is, in many ways, what college football stands for—student-athletes going to college to earn a degree while at the same time playing football, representing their school with character, honor, and hard work.

I was so excited to call that game that I spent the entire week on the road preparing for it. What an amazing week, spending two days in Annapolis with Navy, then two days with Army. Both campuses are beautiful and filled with history.

The game itself is a treat for the purist—starting with the walk-on of both school bands. This is a part of a ceremony that starts well before the two teams go onto the field to warm up. Even in the cold and rain, the bands maintain their military discipline and treat the weather as a nonfactor.

As for the game itself, both teams like to run the ball, creating a good old-fashioned slugfest on the field. It's almost like watching a game before the advent of the forward pass—just old-fashioned blocking, tackling, and hustling.

While these teams seldom have players with the talent or the aspirations to play in the NFL, their desire to compete and win, especially in this game, is second to none. No teams in the country have players who try harder or possess more passion for victory in a rivalry game than you'll see from Army-Navy. I highly recommend attending one of these games.

Auburn-Alabama

Fans and friends ask me all the time what my favorite game is. My standard reply is that if the Lord told me I had one more game I could see before leaving this world, hands down I'd go to the Iron Bowl. Auburn versus Alabama on a Saturday night at either location is phenomenal.

There's no doubt that all rivalry games possess a high level of desire to win by both the teams and their fans. But add to that a genuine hatred among most Tide and Tigers fans, and you've got the makings of a lot of physical confrontations—on the field and off!

One time, while on location at an Iron Bowl game being played in Birmingham, Fowler and I were contemplating whether to go out for dinner the night before the game. We couldn't decide what to do because we knew we didn't want to be surrounded by a bunch of dudes all night asking questions about the next day's game. We found a nice off-the-beaten-path restaurant to hang out in. We were hiding in a corner not getting hounded, at least for a little while. But then we were discovered, and a small group came over and was relentless with their questions. And they were hard-core with their thoughts, more than once questioning us as to why we'd said this or that about their team, Alabama.

Fowler and I looked at each other and just shrugged our shoulders; we knew this was coming.

Guess what?

This small die-hard group was a bunch of young ladies! Not even guys! Man, they love their football down in the great state of Alabama, that's for sure.

Ohio State–Michigan

For those keeping count, I haven't mentioned Ohio State–Michigan. That's because I've seen both teams play in person many times over the years, but I've yet to see an OSU-Michigan game in person. I'm bummed about it, too. It's one of the greatest rivalry games in the country, with tons of passion from players and fans. Maybe I'll get lucky in the broadcast lineup of games and be able to announce one. I've got loads of other rivalries to compare it to.

• • •

Getting back to 2008, the regular season for most teams was out of the way. As we say here in Texas, "The hay was in the barn." Teams had to live (or die) with the results of their actions. The only teams still standing were the ones playing for conference championships—all hoping to win big and move on to the biggest stage of them all: the BCS championship game.

THE BIG ONE

onference Championship Saturday—it's kind of exciting and leads you to believe that there's a mini-tournament going on around the country to see who moves on to bigger and more important games. Well, while the slogan works, the details don't.

Here's what I mean:

Only three of the major conferences hold a conference championship game—the SEC, the ACC, and the Big 12.

The BCS rankings are a combination of three elements, with each counting equally toward the overall standings: (1) the coaches poll, consisting of sixty-one current coaches, (2) the Harris Poll, made up of former coaches and players, and (3) the computers poll, which is an average of six different computer rankings. Simplified: Coaches poll + Harris Poll + Computers poll = Total score for a school. At the end of the regular season, the two highest ranked teams play for the national championship. I highly recommend that all of the major conferences have a conference championship game or none of them do.

Conferences that have the extra game can be blessed or cursed by it. It works nicely for a school that's not in the BCS top-2 rankings at the end of the regular season. That school needs another game against a highly ranked opponent for a victory that could possibly elevate them into the top two and a shot at the national championship.

The following lists created at the end of the 2008 regular season, before the conference title games, show how my ballot differed from the BCS rankings:

Craig James	BCS
1. Alabama	1. Alabama
2. Texas	2. Oklahoma
3. Oklahoma	3. Texas
4. Florida	4. Florida

First, let's take Texas. The Big 12 had the three-way tie between Texas, OU, and Texas Tech in the South division; Missouri had won the North division outright. The Big 12 tiebreaker rule that ultimately decided who would go on to the Big 12 Championship Game went to OU because they were the highest-ranked BCS team at the time, at number 2. Remember back to Thanksgiving weekend when UT beat an unranked, below-average team in Texas A&M? Two days later, OU beat a ranked, solid opponent in Oklahoma State. By virtue of a quality win, OU jumped Texas in the standings and therefore became the highest-ranked BCS team in the Big 12.

Texas Tech, who'd beaten Texas and lost later to OU, was behind both OU and UT in the BCS standings and left out of the conversation altogether. Confusing, isn't it? Stupid, too! The BCS and its ranking system weren't created to help decide conference champions. They were created to try to match up the top two teams in the country at the end of the season.

So OU was set to take on Missouri in the Big 12 Championship Game while Texas stayed at home. Turns out that Missouri should have stayed home. The game wasn't even close. OU thumped the heck out of the Tigers, 62–21. Their convincing win assured the Sooners a spot in the national championship game against the winner of the SEC title game: number-1 Alabama versus number-4 Florida.

Going into this game I also had Florida ranked number 4. So they needed another game to help them climb higher in the polls. Alabama was ranked number 1, so whoever won this game was moving on to Miami for the national championship game regardless.

Alabama-Florida was a matchup of two head coaches who are masterful at both game strategy and head games. Nick Saban had won a national title while head man at LSU and was well on his way to another title shot at Alabama. In just his second year with 'Bama, Saban led his squad to their first undefeated regular season since '94, going 12–0.

I've always admired Saban's ability to recruit hard-core players and the way he almost wills his own personal drive into each of them to make everyone better. Remember that earlier I talked about how powerful a team's desire to win must be; they must have that laser focus and insatiable appetite to win. LSU had it in 2003 when Saban coached the Tigers to a national championship, and I was seeing a similar air of confidence in this '08 Tide team.

Across the field was Urban Meyer, who can be described with the same adjectives. Football guy versus football guy!

Unlike the Big 12 title game, the SEC matchup turned out to be a good football game. The Tide entered as the number-1-ranked team in the country. Florida was ranked number 4 in the BCS polls. 'Bama was undefeated, while Florida had only one early-season loss, to Ole Miss at home.

My pregame evaluation was that Alabama had a lot of young, hard-nosed football players. They didn't have a bunch of individual name stars . . . yet. QB John Parker Wilson was making plays and, more important, *not* making plays for the other team. Bottom line: Alabama just lined up and hit people in the mouth play after play.

On the other hand, Coach Meyer had to handle several egos on his team. He had lots of name guys like Tim Tebow, Percy Harvin, and Brandon Spikes. Thinking back to the spring, when I spent time with the Gators, one of Coach Meyer's goals was to help Spikes evolve into a leader on defense. Meyer knew he had to have a great defense to contend for a title.

Spikes was the best defensive player I saw during my spring tour. After a Gators scrimmage in which he was without question the best player on the field, Coach spent one-on-one time with Spikes after practice trying to convince him that his teammates would accept his "vocal" leadership, too. It was no problem for Spikes to lead by physical example; he'd been doing that with ease. What challenged Spikes was his ability to lead with his words, as well. My observation was that Spikes was liked by his teammates and he didn't want to blow these friendships by jumping on one of 'em for not getting after it. After watching him practice, I could understand and appreciate how he felt.

Some stars are blessed with verbal leadership skills. Tebow, for example, is far more polished—some might call it political—with his prodding. After one play during the spring scrimmage, Spikes got right in the face of the entire offense and challenged any one of them to do something about his dominance. I'm telling ya, not one of those players paused a second to confront the guy.

I see it all the time: a player makes a play then stands over the opponent and talks trash. But what Spikes was doing was different—he wasn't just talking, he was in on darn near every tackle, too. His outburst meant this: "My buddies and me are over here today, and it is going to be *our* day! And there isn't anything you chumps can do about it!" Spikes's tirade *had* to have worked. I mean, I was motivated, and I wasn't even playing.

My guess is that Meyer was encouraging Spikes to continue with what he was doing in practice on the field. When his teammates got to know the type of personality Spikes has, they wouldn't take it personally when he jumped down their throats trying to make 'em better.

It's the delicate matters that separate great coaches from good ones. Very few coaches would recognize a player's situation like the one with Spikes and then counsel that player through the challenge.

I picked Florida to win the SEC championship game because of the overall experience of their leadership guys. My point was well displayed when late in the third quarter Alabama took the lead 20–17. All kinds of momentum was on 'Bama's side, but the Gators calmly went on an eleven-play drive to retake the lead at 24–20, a lead they never surrendered. The final score was Florida 31, Alabama 20.

The stage was set for a battle between the winner of the hottest conference in the country, the Big 12, against the battle-tested and talented Florida Gators.

By the end of the SEC game, most of the Heisman ballots had been mailed in. Over the years, the Heisman Trophy, for me, has lost a lot of its prestige. Don't get me wrong, it's still an honor for a player and his teammates to win the award. My problem is that the award doesn't go to college football's most outstanding player, as it says on the trophy. It more than likely goes to the player whose school had enough money and experience to promote the heck out of their star. That's not right, is it?

In 2007 Darren McFadden, a multiple-threat runner/passer/receiver from the University of Arkansas, was the most outstanding player in college football. I mean no disrespect to what Tim Tebow did to win the Heisman in '07. He had an awesome season, but the most outstanding player in the country was McFadden. The dude ran for 321 yards in a game against a tough

South Carolina defense, as well as led his team to victory over the number-1 team in the country, LSU. In that upset, McFadden carried the ball 32 times for 206 yards. He was a warrior, a beast, a player who reminded me of someone like Vince Young when he was at Texas and could elevate himself above the rest of the players. The problem was that McFadden didn't have enough support around him to play for a national title and therefore didn't get the same national publicity that Tebow did. McFadden did win unanimous All-American honors and even picked up the Doak Walker award in his sophomore and junior years. That award goes to the nation's top running back. McFadden took his hardware on to the NFL, where he continues to shine.

I didn't really start out to vent on the Heisman, but while I'm at it, I think it's important to note that only one defensive player has ever won the award. Charles Woodson of the University of Michigan won it primarily as a defensive back in 1997. I mention this because it supports my position that the award goes to the player with the most highlights on *SportsCenter*. Notice how it's always a running back or a quarterback being shown? No doubt that the winners of the award are darn good. But again, this award states that it's for college football's most outstanding player. If we're honest, we'll admit that there are many *great* and *outstanding* players who don't carry the ball and, so, have no shot at the award. They should rename the award to reflect the reality that it goes to the most talented and publicized runner or thrower in college football.

At any rate, the 2008 season sure did have a lot of front-runners for the award. Early on we thought running back Bennie Wells of Ohio State might win it, but he never broke out. Graham Harrell, QB of Texas Tech, had an outstanding season, but his Red Raiders lost on national TV late in the season, and he never got respect from that point on.

A little education before I say who won and how I voted: the Heisman voters are split into six regions with 145 media voters per region. Previous winners have a vote, too, bringing the total voters to roughly 900. Each voter lists three candidates in order of preference. The top guy gets three points, second place gets two, and third choice gets one. The top total vote-getter wins.

In an extremely close vote, the 2008 Heisman winner was Sam Bradford, QB of OU. Bradford totaled 1,726 points; Colt McCoy placed second with 1,604 points; Tim Tebow came in third with 1,575.

In truth, there were several players in '08 for whom you could have built a case as to why they should've won the award. For example, Graham Harrell led the Texas Tech Red Raiders to a school-best eleven-win season. In doing so, Harrell passed for nearly 5,000 yards. Those are major accomplishments and numbers for Harrell and his school.

Here are my top three votes for the 2008 Heisman Trophy:

First Place: Colt McCoy

I put Colt at the top of the list because there's no way UT would have won eleven regular-season games without him. He led his team in rushing with 561 yards and 11 touchdowns, but also went nuts in the passing game. Colt's completion percentage of 77.6 percent was amazing. And I personally saw that many of his incompletions were balls intentionally thrown away by him or ones that were dropped by a receiver. Colt totaled 3,445 yards with 32 TD passes and only 7 interceptions. In not just my opinion but also that of many other experts, including UT head coach Mack Brown, Colt put up his lofty numbers without as many talented and experienced teammates as his competitors had. Both Tebow and Bradford had more around them to help them out. Plus, I thought back to my spring tour visit to Texas, and my takeaway was that they'd lose as many as three or four games in '08. Even Colt didn't predict the kind of season he or his team would have.

Second Place: Sam Bradford

Sam Bradford is one of the best pure QBs I've watched play college football. By *pure* I mean a QB who is traditional in his approach to the game. He drops back in the pocket, makes his reads, then delivers the ball to an open receiver. Sam's accuracy and poise are amazing. I've seen him throw a bullet to a receiver between two close defenders, then loft a lazy pass just over the outstretched arms of a defender right into the hands of his receiver. Sam's athletic ability allows him to move in the pocket to buy time for his receivers to get open. Sam had gaudy numbers of more than 4,000 yards passing, with 46 TDs to only 6 interceptions. He didn't get my first-place vote because I thought he had more talent to work with than McCoy. And that doesn't mean that I don't think Sam isn't an unbelievable person and player. Bradford will be fun to watch in his senior season in '09! No doubt, I think Sam's the hands-down favorite for the Heisman in 2009.

Third Place: Tim Tebow

Tim would tell you in a New York second that winning the national championship was far more important to him than winning another Heisman. Tebow will go down as one of college football's greatest players. He's the warrior I described earlier in the book, with personal class and integrity that are even better than his football skills. If there ever was a poster boy for college football it would have to be Tim Tebow. As with Bradford, I thought Tim's surrounding talent was far greater than McCoy's—hence my reason for the order of the placement of these players on my ballot.

• • •

Forget the individual stuff. The 2008 season was all about which team would win the national championship!

I wasn't surprised in the least that Oklahoma and Florida ended up playing for the national championship. Based on what I'd seen in the spring from these two, it was clear they had the coaching *and* the talent. And both schools had a premier QB to lead them. Going back to the spring and my post-scrimmage visit with Coach Meyer, I think he knew that day that if his defense played the '08 season with as much passion and desire as he got from them on that warm April day, his Gators were going to be hard to beat.

Same with Stoops: his confidence coming out of the spring and his belief in his players were evident in the way he talked about them. Like Meyer, Stoops had won a national championship, too, back in 2000 with the Sooners. So he knew what it took to get into the title game. What stood out for me while watching the Sooners work out was how well coached they were—and, boy, did they look good in pads.

When I analyze a big game, I look at many factors before deciding who I think will win.

Character

How has a team handled adversity over the course of the season? Did they respond to a loss well? How did they handle the loss of key players to injury?

Florida showed me a lot after their loss to Ole Miss. It would have been understandable if they'd lost that little edge needed to stay focused on a daily basis. And with the Gators on the front end of their tough SEC schedule, anything short of total focus would have greatly increased their chance for another loss. But Tim Tebow's postgame declaration after the Ole Miss loss seemed to rally his teammates and coaches to stay the course. I'm sure Coach Meyer reminded his team that it was a long season and that if they won out, they'd be in the SEC title game with a shot at the conference title. And history has proven that the strength and respect of the conference have been enough to place their champions in the national championship game.

OU did the same after their loss in October to Texas. The Sooners not only went on a winning streak, they did it in a big way, scoring what seemed to be 60 points a game. I remember sitting at the studio desk in New York one Saturday wanting to hear a first-person account from a coach who'd played OU about how they were doing. Art Briles was in his first year as the Baylor Bears' coach, and he told me that what most impressed him about OU was the way they carried themselves on the field. In other words, OU was big and powerful and, as Art said, they had a calm confidence about them.

To me, this category was a tie—no advantage to either team.

Coaching

I also put this down as a push between Coach Meyer and Coach Stoops. As I've said, I admire both men, including how intensely focused they are getting their teams ready to play. Both also have the experience of winning a title, so this wasn't going to be either's first rodeo.

Third Downs

Which team is better at getting their opponents off the field on third down? No question for me that Florida had the advantage. It's not that OU was bad on third down, but I felt that Florida was a little better. Every great defense has the ability to suck it up on third down; somebody comes up with a play to get their opponent's offense off the field. I find that the teams that are the best in this category are those with the best athletes capable of playing in space—that is, guys who can run and defend the pass or options in open areas.

I gave Florida the edge.

Battle-Tested

I've always been a big believer that you have to play the best to be the best. In games against excellent competition, coaches and players are better able to discover their strengths and weaknesses. The best conference in my opinion during 2008 was the Big 12, so I knew that OU had been tested, especially their defense. The Big 12 had a ton of great QBs, as many lumped in one conference as I'd ever seen.

I got a call one week in November from my friend Bob Tebow, father of superman Tim, asking what I thought of the Big 12 defenses. I told him I thought they were good—maybe not UF- or Alabama-good, but good. I chuckle now at Bob's question because I think he was working me in a sly way to suggest that the Big 12 QB numbers were slightly better than his son's numbers because of the average defenses in the Big 12.

As for Florida, I never for a second wondered if they'd been battle-tested. You don't win the SEC without having your character tested weekly.

I considered this category another tie.

Quarterbacks

Every time I'm stumped and undecided on which team to pick, I look at how the two QBs have played. Who do I think is playing better? This was a tough call. Both Bradford and Tebow are spectacular, so I got no help from this category, either. Once again. it was a tie.

• • •

So it turns out that the main reason I expected Florida to win was because the game was being played in Miami; it wasn't Gainesville, but it was still a home game for the Gators—a big plus. If the game had been played in Norman, Oklahoma, I'd have picked OU.

Before kickoff I got a call from my Thursday night partner (and former Gator), Erin Andrews. EA was on her way to the game, but was stuck in traffic and nervous for her Gators. We weren't covering the game. It was on Fox, so it was okay for her to be just a fan of her alma mater. I bring up Erin's nerves—although she worries about every game—because I kept hearing from lots of Gators fans that they were nervous about playing OU. I'm convinced a lot of those worries were because they didn't really know whether the Big 12 was good or not. Was it a conference full of pass-happy offenses with no defenses? Or did they have a bunch of solid teams, which would mean that their Sooners were the real deal? While the Florida fans might have been unsure of how talented OU was, I guarantee you that the Gators football team knew what to expect: a big, fast, and talented OU machine.

Early in the game, Gators fans got their answer: the Sooners were for real. Both teams came into the game scoring points as if they were going against air. UF was averaging 45 a game while the Sooners were putting up 54. Crazy—and even crazier when after the first quarter the game was a scoreless tie.

OU's defense had made a statement that they could play, and so had Florida's. The second quarter was telling. The score was tied at 7 going to halftime. But Florida had dodged a major bullet not once but twice. OU was stopped on fourth and goal from the 1-yard line; later, OU threw a goal-line interception with 6 seconds to go. OU had its foot on the throat of the Gators defense, and yet the Gators found a way to keep 'em out of the end zone—twice!

Remember how I categorized character, winning third downs, and being battle-tested? Tell me they didn't come into evaluation in that second quarter!

Entering the fourth quarter, the score was tied at 14. This was a great game, and it was setting up to be a perfect ending to the '08 season.

A key player in this game was UF all-purpose player Percy Harvin. Harvin was battling what was reported to be a high ankle sprain entering the game. Harvin is one of those rare players who can do a little bit of everything. His speed is his number-one asset, and based on how he was playing in this title game, that ankle injury was doing just fine. For the game, Harvin had 9 carries for 122 yards to go along with 5 catches for 49 yards. His speed was unmatched by anybody on OU's defense.

Remember what I said about the importance of third downs? Harvin and his Gators' offense were hard to stop on third down. UF was a remarkable 12 for 17 (compared to OU's 6 for 13). That's a huge conversion rate, which allowed Florida to go on to not only score points but to keep Sam Bradford and his OU offense on the sidelines. I also thought that Tebow's ability to run against the Sooners was critical. During the game, and especially late in the game, Tebow seemed to take his competitiveness to another level. He bulled his way into OU's defense time and again. At the end, the Gators had outrushed the Sooners 249 to 107 yards.

In the fourth quarter, Florida kicked a field goal then scored a touchdown to win the game 24–14 and become national champs for the second time in three years. And Tebow's postgame vow after the Ole Miss loss to lead his team to victory for the rest of the season was fulfilled.

• • •

The calendar year of 2008 was easily the most enjoyable of any I've covered. No doubt a big reason was because my spring tour was so successful. I learned so much more about the schools, the teams, the players, and the coaches. I can't wait for the 2009 season, which has the potential to be the best of all time.

Why? College football was given a special treat when several of the '08 superstars decided to return for their senior seasons. Instead of moving on to the NFL, these young men will return for one more run. Tip your hats to Tim Tebow, Sam Bradford, Colt McCoy, and other All-Americans whose decisions to return will no doubt make 2009 memorable.

Take care, and I'll see ya at the games! God bless us all.

INDEX

DISCARD

10/09